Media Skills for Middle Schools

TEACHING LIBRARY MEDIA RESEARCH AND INFORMATION SKILLS SERIES

Edited by Paula Kay Montgomery

Library Media Skills: Strategies for Instructing Primary Students. By Alice R. Seaver.

Media Skills for Middle Schools: Strategies for Library Media Specialists and Teachers. By Lucille W. Van Vliet.

Ready for Reference: Media Skills for Intermediate Students. By Barbara Bradley Zlotnick.

MEDIA SKILLS
FOR MIDDLE SCHOOLS

Strategies for
Library Media Specialists
and Teachers

LUCILLE W. VAN VLIET

EDITED BY
PAULA KAY MONTGOMERY

1984
Libraries Unlimited, Inc.
Littleton, Colorado

LIBRARIES UNLIMITED, INC.
P.O. Box 263
Littleton, Colorado 80160-0263

Library of Congress Cataloging in Publication Data

Van Vliet, Lucille W., 1926-
    Media skills for middle schools.

    (Teaching library media research and information
skills series)
    Bibliography: p. 247
    Filmography: p. 249
    1. School libraries (Elementary school)--Activity
programs.   2. Instructional materials centers.
3. Media programs (Education)   4. Audio-visual library
service.   I. Montgomery, Paula Kay.   II. Title.
III. Series.
Z675.S3V34   1984   027.8'222   84-3926
ISBN 0-87287-410-9

Table
of Contents

Part II

Foreword

Preparing middle school students for attaining those skills necessary for a successful academic career and for lifelong learning is a challenge to any teacher or library media specialist. This challenge asserts itself because of the many physical and emotional changes going on with students as they matriculate through the grades. This book, *Media Skills for Middle Schools*, has been developed as part of the series, *Teaching Library Media Research and Information Skills*, to examine the most productive methods for teaching those essential library media skills at the middle school level.

Media Skills for Middle Schools presents an integrated approach to the teaching of library media and research skills. With this approach, the library media specialist and teacher are partners in the delivery of instruction to students. This instruction may be provided in a variety of ways by either one of the instructors. It is a normal outcome of the unified library media concept. Students learn from a variety of formats in situations that are meaningful to them. This book provides a model for this type of instruction and identifies more than seventy sample learning situations that might be of use to the middle school teacher and library media specialist.

The author focuses on integrating library media skill instruction into all areas of the curriculum. She gives attention to the efforts needed to plan with teachers. She shows specific examples of support of the principal and tools for planning. The major strengths of the book are the sample lessons and units of instruction. Each lesson or unit prescribes the content and library media skill objectives to be taught. The learning situation, materials and resources, and activities are provided. Reproducible activity worksheets appear throughout. Among the most helpful ideas are the suggestions for roles to be played by both teacher and library media specialist. The reader will find a balance in situations where the teacher and library media specialist play varied roles in teaching. The author is careful to spell out the assessment to be used.

The book has been written by a library media specialist with over twenty years of experience at the junior high and middle school level. She has put these ideas into practice in a most successful manner, and she has earned the admiration and respect of her students and the school faculty, Hammond Middle School, Howard County Public Schools, Ellicott City, Maryland. In 1980, Lucille Van Vliet received the Mae I. Graham Award from the Maryland Educational Media Organization for Outstanding Media Program of the Year. It is an award well deserved.

This book should prove to be of assistance to new library media specialists beginning work in middle schools, to teachers and library media specialists looking for successful models for emulation, and for any library media professional searching for ideas that will assist in incorporating research skills into the classroom.

Paula Kay Montgomery

Preface

Media Skills for Middle Schools: Strategies for Library Media Specialists and Teachers is designed to promote the teaching of library media skills as an integral part of the school curriculum. It is intended to be used as a springboard for the development of an integrated library media skills program based on the philosophy, goals, and curriculum in individual schools.

The principles of middle school educational philosophy and characteristics of middle school students as set forth in Part I provide the groundwork for the 70 sample lessons in Part II.

This book is the product of many people who have contributed to the development and implementation of the library media skills program at Hammond Middle School in Howard County, Maryland. A special recognition goes to the teachers, administrators, and staff of Hammond Middle School for the years 1971-1983.

Shirley Ashcraft	Eugene Estes
Donna Ball	Ellen Feldman
Wayne Binder	Linda Feldmesser
Roberta Breslow	James Griffin
Dottie Brill	Maureen Grimes
Jacqueline Brown	Ann Hogg
Albertha Caldwell	Mimi Hopkins
Christine Carew	Jo Ann Hutchens
Nancy Chen	Mary Jennings
Lorna Chestnutt	Terry Johnson
Joanna Cooper	Phillip Kimball
Herbert Cottrell	Brina Krupp
Herbert Cross	Carolyn Lanier
Wayne Danley	Trish Lavin
Susan Deemer	Adrienne Lichtinger
James DeGeorge	Gloria Liggins

David Lovewell

Sharon Manning

Midge McClure

Louise McDaniels

Irma Jean McNelia

Debra Miller

David Oaks

Ella O'Colman

Rick Oursler

Tom Payne

E. Joseph Picek

Nick Rangos

Pat Rees

Nancy Rhead

Hob Shry

Roma Slyter

Mary Smith

Anna Spring

Cindy Thompson

Tom Thrasher

Wanser Turner

Marilyn Walt

Phyllis Weller

Kathy Yerep

Appreciation goes to the following people for their special roles in the production of this book:

Dr. James DiVirgilio

Joseph Duckworth

Timothy Gaither

Dr. Mary Hovet

William Kerewsky

Dr. James Liesener

Alfreda Martino

Celeste Smalkin

John Soles

Donnadine Spilman

Dr. H. Thomas Walker

Estelle Williamson

In addition, special thanks go to the following:

Judy Busse for graphics

Helen McLaughlin for typing and editing

Paula Montgomery for assistance and suggestions

Robert Van Vliet and our children Jo Ann and Alan for support and encouragement

Grateful acknowledgment is given to Dr. M. Thomas Goedeke, Superintendent of Howard County Public Schools, Ellicott City, Maryland, to the Board of Education of Howard County, and to the Citizens' Ad Hoc Committee to Study Middle Schools for permission to use curriculum guides and committee reports in the preparation of lessons.

PART I
Library Media Skills
in Middle Schools

Middle School Students

1

The Middle School

DEFINITION

The middle school is a uniquely designed transitional school that provides for the education of early adolescents between elementary school and high school. Based on the nature and developmental needs of these students in transition, or *transescents,* the middle school ideally supplies a suitable environment for the eleven- to fourteen-year-old student. A student-centered program offers the opportunity for academic, personal, and social growth.

The middle school movement gained momentum during the 1960s as educators became increasingly dissatisfied with the junior high school. Many people felt that the junior high school was not accomplishing the purpose for which it was originally intended. That purpose was to provide a school especially for the young adolescent. Little was done to prepare special courses of study based on the learning requirements of early adolescents. Some junior high schools had become a mere imitation of the senior high school in instructional methods, curriculum, and social activities. The inclusion of the ninth grade in the junior high school necessitated providing courses for secondary school credit. The organizational pattern of junior high schools did not contain those pupils of compatible physical, social, and emotional maturation. A number of school districts chose to abandon the junior high in favor of some type of middle school.[1]

The middle school concept was promoted in the 1960s and 1970s by prominent educators such as William Alexander, Mary Compton, Donald Eichorn, Paul S. George, John H. Lounsbury, Conrad E. Toepfer, Jr., Gordon Vars, and Emmett Williams. Their ideas on the philosophy, goals, and program had a profound impact on the development and growth of middle schools.

Many other educators contributed to the middle school movement through books, journal articles, research studies, and conference reports. They stressed the need for a student-centered school developed along a pattern that would serve students who have similar intellectual, physical, and emotional needs. Of special significance was the organization of the National Middle School Association, which holds an annual middle school conference and publishes the *Middle School Journal, Middle School Research Studies*, and a number of professional books.

The growth of middle schools has been phenomenal with current estimates ranging from 8,000 to 10,000 schools. The organizational structure varies, but the most common organization is for grades 6-8. Other patterns include grades 7-8 and 5-8.

Just as some of the middle schools vary in organizational structure, some of the middle schools vary in implementation of an exemplary middle school program; however, the middle school concept offers many possibilities for achieving the mission assigned to it.

PHILOSOPHY AND GOALS

The philosophy of a middle school must be derived from the overall philosophy of the educational system of which it is a part. The broad statement of beliefs subscribed to by many educational systems include such important concepts relevant to middle schools as to develop self-potential, to achieve success, to understand themselves and others, to achieve proficiency in the basic skills, to respect the dignity of work, to grow in the range of cognitive abilities, to respect all individuals, to become responsible citizens, to obtain the skills needed for effective living, and to develop lifelong interests for leisure activities.

The paramount goal of a middle school is to provide programs designed specifically to meet the physical, social, emotional, and intellectual needs of young adolescents. These programs should be student centered and activity oriented with clearly defined measurable objectives.

In support of this goal, a middle school should strive to

1. Initiate a continuous progress program allowing students to move at their own individual rate toward the mastery of skills.

2. Provide training for middle school teachers to help them understand their role as middle school educators.

3. Promote an outstanding library media program as an integral part of the total school program.

4. Provide a wide assortment of instructional activities such as games, field trips, festivals, and audiovisual projects.

5. Teach students basic process skills.

6. Strive to develop higher level thinking skills in students.

7. Provide for flexible scheduling and flexible grouping of students.

8. Use a variety of learning materials and strategies.

9. Promote team planning and team teaching of interdisciplinary units.

10. Include a strong program of health and physical education.

11. Provide for remedial instruction.

12. Promote ideas that involve students in exploration and discovery.

13. Plan programs of study for the gifted and talented.

14. Emphasize the development of communication skills.

15. Plan continuous methods of evaluation and reporting.

16. Involve students in coeducational programs in home economics and industrial arts.

17. Provide instruction and enrichment activities in art and music.

18. Institute an advisor/advisee program.

19. Provide a well-developed guidance program for individual and group guidance.

20. Accept the differences in each student.

21. Initiate a special interest or activities program for students.

22. Provide many opportunities for students to interact with peers.

23. Help students develop a commitment to their own education.

24. Provide social experiences designed for middle school students.

25. Allow students the opportunity to develop creativity and self-expression.

26. Emphasize the development of responsibility, self-respect, and self-discipline.

27. Provide an extensive intramural sports program.

28. Plan the articulation process between the grade levels in middle school as well as between the elementary and high schools.

29. Provide for use of innovative programs and new technology.

30. Promote a strong PTA organization involving the parents and community.[2]

STAFF MEMBERS

The implementation of the goals of a middle school is the joint responsibility of the staff of the school system and the individual school. All staff members involved with middle schools should be committed to the middle school concept and should understand the needs and capabilities of middle school students.

The members of the board of education, the superintendent, the assistant superintendent, the director of middle schools, and the supervisors and specialists play key roles in providing policies, services, financial support, lists of appropriate texts and materials, curriculum guides, and workshops. They also assist in the improvement of instruction by direct involvement in the instructional program.

Additional school system resources include human relations services, pupil personnel workers, psychological services, research and development services, and staff development services.

The success of the program of a middle school depends ultimately on the effectiveness and commitment of the staff. The principal and assistant principal provide the leadership to design a viable organization for the instructional program. They formulate and implement policies and procedures, coordinate school activities, and provide a continuous assessment of the program. By creating a communications network with the staff, students, parents, and community, they can involve these groups in the decision-making process.

A well-prepared, cooperative teaching staff participates in program planning and evaluation. They strive to use the teaching strategies that meet the needs of middle school students by emphasizing process skills and activity-oriented experiences.

The guidance counselor coordinates programs dealing with the affective needs of students and plans individual and group guidance activities. The counselor is also responsible for promoting career awareness and improving human relations.

The library media specialist participates in the instructional program of the school by collaborating with teachers in the teaching of library media skills objectives as an integral part of the curriculum. As a teacher, library media center administrator, and provider of services, the library media specialist contributes to the total school program.

A courteous, friendly, and helpful secretarial and custodial staff who relate to middle school students can provide many services to ensure the efficient operation of the school.

CURRICULUM

The middle school curriculum varies according to school systems and individual schools; however, many middle schools use a developmental skills program as a broad general base for the education of all students.

The following is a sample of a middle school curriculum from the Howard County Public School System in Maryland.[3]

A Middle School Curriculum

Art

Formal elements of art and composition
Composition
Seeing
Enjoying
Creating art forms
Career concepts

Foreign Language

Introductory experience:
  Conversation
  Communication
English for Speakers of Other Languages
Development of functional skills in English
Career concepts

Health

First Aid
Fitness
Nutrition
Diseases
Assimilated substances:
  Alcohol, Tobacco, Drugs
Family life and human development
Career concepts

Home Economics

Programs for strengthening family life
Food and nutrition
Clothing and textiles
Home furnishings
Home management
Consumer education
Career concepts

Industrial Arts

Qualities of good design and construction
Sketching, drawing, planning, production
Woodworking, leathercraft, plastics
Proper use of tools
Career concepts

Language Arts

Continuous progress program in literature,
  composition, and spoken arts
Career concepts

Math

Continuous progress/appropriate placement
General math
Algebra
Geometry
Computer literacy
Accelerated/advanced courses
Career concepts

Music

Music literacy:
  Reader
  Writer
  Performer
  Consumer
Chorus
Instrumental:
  Band
  Strings
Career concepts

Physical Education

Sequential program:
  Team sports
  Individual sports
Water safety
Intramurals
Career concepts

Reading

Developmental:
  Sight vocabulary
  Functional word attack skills
  Comprehension skills
  Interest in reading
Challenge:
  Higher level thinking processes
  Enjoyment of reading
Corrective:
  Diagnostic and prescriptive
Career concepts

Social Studies

Prepare students for productive and effective citizenship
Foster positive attitude:
  Belief in democratic government
  Dignity and self-worth of individual
  Equality of opportunity
Skills:
  Maps and globes
  Research and problem solving
  Interpersonal
Career concepts

Science

Activity oriented:
  General science
  Life science
  Physical science
Laboratory safety
Laboratory experiments
Observation techniques
Tools of science
Metric system
Career concepts

Adapted from *Middle School Handbook,* Howard County Public School System, Ellicott City, Maryland 21043. Reprinted by permission.

SPECIALIZED PROGRAMS AND ACTIVITIES

The regular instructional program of a middle school may be enhanced by specialized programs and activities. A program for the gifted and talented can provide many opportunities for students with exceptional potential to participate in varied activities related to academics or the performing arts. A special education program for students with learning or behavior deviations can provide special services and instruction by placing students in the proper learning environment based on the needs of each student.

A program of independent study emphasizes the student's role in developing personal competencies by allowing the student to select and plan a course of study or project in a special field of interest. A teacher serves as a consultant or advisor. The organizational structure, types of programs, reporting, and supervision may vary.

Another program designed to meet the special interests of students and to provide an introduction to a wide range of activities is the minicourse, club, or special activities program. Students and teachers can interact in a non-academic setting and share happy rewarding experiences in such activities as Chinese cooking, bridge, chess, models, photography, reading, computer games, and acrobic dancing.

The advisor/advisee or homeroom program is essential to the development of interpersonal skills. It helps to build a closer relationship between teachers and students, students and peers, and students and family. It offers many students a caring environment where they can identify their strengths and weaknesses, learn to better understand themselves and their peers, communicate effectively, and make appropriate decisions.

Appropriate social activities for middle schools allow for the diversity of development of middle school students. As students participate in field trips, concerts, and festivals, they have the opportunity to socialize with one another. Multipurpose parties with games, dancing, and movies provide choices for students. Middle school students love to eat; therefore, a wide assortment of food should be a part of each party.

The sports program of a middle school includes a basic skills program in the physical education curriculum and a well-planned intramural program. Intramurals usually take place immediately after school. Some schools provide an activity bus two days a week for a small fee to encourage student participation. Some of the successful intramurals include roller skating, basketball, bowling, gymnastics, volleyball, soccer, hockey, wrestling, and softball. Middle school teachers from many disciplines should be encouraged to sponsor intramurals.

The facilities for a middle school should be appropriate for the program and goals of that school; however, the facilities do not make the program. Traditional buildings can house an exemplary middle school program; innovative open space buildings can house a traditional program. Ideally, the facilities for an exemplary program provide for flexible grouping. Moveable partitions help to provide this flexibility. Special planning is needed to accommodate laboratories for science, home economics, industrial arts, foreign language, remedial subjects, and computers. Study carrels throughout the school offer places for independent study.

It is important for the library media center to be accessible to all parts of the school. Adequate space is needed for reading, listening, viewing, studying, teaching, planning, and producing audiovisual programs.

Exhibits, displays, learning centers, and decorations contribute to the atmosphere of middle schools. Students respond to bright and cheerful surroundings.

ORGANIZATIONAL PATTERN

The organizational pattern of a middle school determines the educational program. Some form of teaming is basic to the middle school concept. Team teaching allows for a flexible process of grouping students for instruction by two or more teachers who plan together the specific objectives and activities. Teams may be organized as disciplinary, interdisciplinary, or a combination of the two. Using guidelines from the school system, the principal and staff jointly plan for the use of space, time, and personnel. A flexible schedule is necessary to accommodate team teaching, independent study, advisory groups, minicourses, and many other activities.

The teaching strategies in a middle school include a wide variety of methods that allow for student activity, movement, and interaction. Successful strategies employ learning centers, games, field trips, experiments, lectures, demonstrations, role playing, and programmed instruction.

Evaluation is a necessary part of the program of a middle school. The teacher uses easily measureable objectives to assess the student's progress or performance according to the student's ability. This progress is reported to parents through report cards, conferences, telephone calls, and efficiency-deficiency reports. Students are taught self-assessment procedures and are encouraged to communicate with teachers concerning grades and evaluations. Special recognition and encouragement is given to students by displaying their work, giving certificates, congratulating them, and announcing a special honor. Pictures of students who are selected as chef-of-the-week, super-reader, or media quiz winners can be posted on a bulletin board.

The observation and evaluation of all middle school teachers and staff serves to focus on the attainment of goals and objectives. Periodically, all staff members should be a part of a schoolwide assessment of the philosophy, goals, and program of the school.

An exemplary middle school can only be achieved through the joint efforts of a dedicated staff, informed parents, an involved community, and receptive students.

NOTES

[1] Donald Eichorn, "Planning Programs for Transescents" (Paper presented at the University of New York at Buffalo, 17 October 1968), 1-3.

[2] John Lounsbury, Jean V. Marani, and Mary F. Compton, *The Middle School in Profile* (Fairborn, Ohio: National Middle School Association, 1980), 67-71.

[3] Howard County Public Schools, *Middle School Handbook* (Ellicott City, Md.: Howard County Public School System, 1982), 17-37.

BIBLIOGRAPHY

Alexander, William M., and Paul S. George. *The Exemplary Middle School.* New York: Holt, Rinehart and Winston, 1981.

Compton, Mary F. "The Middle School: A Status Report." *Middle School Journal* 7 (June 1976): 3-5.

DiVirgilio, James. "Reflections of Curriculum Needs for Middle Schools." *Education* 92 (April 1972): 78-79.

Epstein, Herman T., and Conrad F. Toepfer, Jr. "Reorganizing Middle Grades Education." *Educational Digest* 44 (October 1978): 10-12.

Grooms, Ann. *Perspectives on the Middle Schools.* Columbus, Ohio: Charles Merrill Co., 1967.

Howard County Public Schools. *Middle School Handbook.* Ellicott City, Md.: Howard County Public School System, 1982.

Kerewsky, William. "Middle Schools." *Maryland Congress of PTA, Inc.* 5 (February 1978): 2. Bulletin.

Kindred, Leslie, Rita J. Wolotkiewicz, John M. Mickelson, Leonard Coplein, Ernest Dyson. *The Middle School Curriculum: A Practitioner's Handbook.* 2d ed. Boston: Allyn and Bacon, 1981.

Leeper, R. R., ed. *Middle School in the Making.* Washington, D. C.: Association for Supervision and Curriculum Development, 1974.

Lounsbury, John H., and Gordon Vars. *A Curriculum for the Middle School Years.* New York: Harper and Row, 1977.

Lounsbury, John H., Jean V. Marani, and Mary F. Compton. *The Middle School in Profile: A Day in the Seventh Grade.* Fairborn, Ohio: National Middle School Association, 1980.

Madon, Constant. "The Middle School: Its Philosophy and Purpose." *Clearing House* 10 (February 1966): 329-30.

Popper, Samuel. *The American Middle School.* Waltham, Mass.: Blaisdell Publishing Company, 1967.

Williams, Emmett L. "What about the Junior High and Middle School?" *NAASP Bulletin* 52 (May 1968): 126-34.

2

The Middle School Student

CHARACTERISTICS

The middle school student is a person who requires a special depth of understanding and acceptance. This student is in transition, on the threshold of adulthood. Each student has a unique pattern of physical, social, emotional, and intellectual growth. These differences are reflected in the varied interests, abilities, attitudes, and social and emotional adjustments of each individual. Educators need to understand the complexities of this age group to provide for the personal and academic needs of each transescent.

The physical characteristics of middle school students show a wide assortment of maturation rates; however, students are maturing at an earlier age than a generation ago. Physiological changes transform the child into an adult. Girls usually reach menarche between the ages of eleven and fifteen. Their period of rapid growth begins around age ten, peaks around age twelve, and declines around age fifteen. Boys generally reach puberty between the ages of thirteen and fifteen. Their growth spurt begins around age eleven or twelve, peaks around fourteen, and declines gradually between the ages of seventeen and twenty. This diversity in maturation creates marked differences in size and maturity between girls and boys during the middle school years.[1]

Most middle school students are restless, tire easily, and may overexert. They may be awkward, clumsy, and have a lack of coordination. Physiological changes can cause students to work less efficiently. Studies by leading educators indicate that brain growth reaches a plateau.[2]

The uneven growth patterns of students often affect their self-image. This is especially true for the students who develop very early or very late. Because they become confused about their physical changes, students need to be taught about body systems and human development.

Middle school students are very concerned about their physical appearance. They desire to be exactly like their peers and are constantly comparing themselves with others. A skin blemish, a scar, or the gaining of a few pounds can be devastating to their ego. Their level of maturity is often erroneously judged by their physical appearance.

The social characteristics of middle school students indicate their desire to understand themselves and their relationship with peers, teachers, and parents. Students ask themselves: Who am I? How do I compare with others? Why am I different? What do others like/dislike about me? Do I belong? Why are friends so changeable? Do my teachers like me? Why do they pick on me? Why are my parents so hard to please? Students are frequently troubled by their assessment of answers to these questions.

Middle school students need recognition and acceptance by their peers. Belonging to a group provides high self-esteem; not belonging to a group produces low self-esteem and dejection. Students tend to accept peer group values and standards. Friendship is very changeable as students are in and out of favor almost daily. Best friends who are inseparable one day may not be on speaking terms the next day. Middle school students enjoy socializing with their peers. They enjoy parties, dancing, and activities that allow them to interact. Generally girls become interested in boys long before boys are interested in them. Peer pressure is a strong motivating force for the middle school student.

A great many middle school students want social interaction with teachers and other staff members. They want to talk about their problems, concerns, successes, failures, and goals. They want support, acceptance, and special considerations. They enjoy meeting with staff members on an informal basis at parties, club activities, homebase programs, lunch, intramurals, and field trips. Students who display antisocial behavior toward staff members are often seeking special attention. Positive interactions between students and teachers can help to promote better relationships.

A transition takes place in the family relationships of middle school students. Students become more independent and are able to stay away from home for longer periods of time. They resist parental guidance and authority. They feel their parents do not understand or appreciate them. They feel their parents put too much emphasis on grades. Parents often feel their sons or daughters are moody, impatient, impulsive, demanding, lazy, and sloppy. If there are brothers and sisters, they tease, fight, and argue. Many times there are changes in the family status that greatly affect the middle school student. Parents should try to build a sense of family togetherness where there is mutual love, respect, communication, and understanding.

The emotional characteristics of middle school students reflect the changeable nature of transescents. On the one hand, they are likeable, cooperative, responsible, sensitive, and trusting. They show interest, motivation, and ingenuity. On the other hand, they are disagreeable, troublesome, egocentric, and avoid responsibility. They can also be prejudiced, insensitive, and intolerant. They may demonstrate erratic and inconsistent behavior and boredom. These characteristics underline the students' need for approval, acceptance, and self-confidence.

The intellectual characteristics of middle school students indicate the wide range of cognitive functions among students. Students move from the level of concrete operations through transitional operations to formal operations. Students progress through these thinking processes on their own timetable. Concrete thinkers focus on the tangible usually ignoring inferences, assumptions, and systematic methods. Transitional thinkers are able to handle more abstract ideas while still relying on some concrete experiences. Formal thinkers can deal with abstract concepts, problem solving, the scientific method, sequences, and long-range planning. The middle school should provide a flexible, continuous progress program to help meet the students' intellectual abilities.

NEEDS

Middle school students have many personal needs. They need to be accepted as individuals, to be themselves, to be treated fairly, and to be heard. They also need affection, security, understanding, approval, acceptance, and moral support from teachers, family, and peers. Their needs include a sense of belonging and nurturing. Teachers and other staff members can provide guidance in helping students to become responsible for self-development.

Middle school students have many academic needs. Since they become bored with routine assignments and drill, activities that allow manipulation and movement are very desirable. Middle school students need trial and error situations where grading is not a factor. Because they are curious and inquisitive, middle school students enjoy opportunities to experiment and time to explore and discover. They should be challenged to stretch their imagination, to develop creativity, and to increase self-expression. By interacting with peers, middle school students try out new ideas and strategies and search to find their own answers. Opportunities for success, recognition, and rewards are an important part of the middle school students' academic life.[3]

The middle school student can successfully make the transition through the stages of pre-adolescence to adolescence by working with teachers and parents to achieve realistic goals.

THE SIXTH-GRADE STUDENT

Sixth-grade students are known as the little kids to seventh- and eighth-grade students. Many remarks are made about their babyish looks or actions. While there are individual differences in the rate of physical maturation, sixth-grade students are noticeably smaller in stature and less mature than other middle school students. Interest in personal appearance, styles, and fads becomes pronounced during this period. Peer pressures are very strong. The intellectual development of sixth-grade students varies from concrete to abstract levels of thinking. Involvement in active games, sports, and laboratory experiments helps to provide outlets for the boundless energy of most sixth-grade students. Some students are insatiable readers, while others are addicted to television viewing; yet, most sixth-grade students enjoy hearing a story that is read or told to them.

Library media skills lessons for sixth-grade students must provide activities that enable students to become independent users of the library media center. Special attention should be given to orientation, equipment operation, development of basic reference skills, introduction to computers, reading guidance, and basic principles of production.

THE SEVENTH-GRADE STUDENT

Seventh-grade students are "in the middle." Their physical, social, emotional, and intellectual development is between later childhood and adolescence. The girls are usually taller and larger than the boys at this age. Seventh-grade students exhibit erratic behavior that results from their mood changes. They are talkative, restless, and impatient. They are also delightful, fun-loving, and humorous. They have a strong desire for approval and acceptance. Peer pressures continue to be very strong. Friends are very important to them.

As they progress toward mastery of some basic skills, they desire opportunities to express originality. They like to participate in games and contests. Many seventh-grade students enjoy working in small groups to prepare group projects or audiovisual productions. Festivals, celebrations, and field trips are fun activities for seventh graders. Reading for pleasure reaches new heights; book selection is fostered by book talks, peer suggestions, teacher suggestions, and specialized bibliographies.

Library media skills lessons for seventh-grade students should provide an extension of the basic reference skills developed in grade six. The lessons should offer opportunities for independent research, the use of special indexes, locating and selecting references for specific purposes, interpreting data, refining bibliographic skills, book selection, and the use of advanced techniques for audio-visual production.

THE EIGHTH-GRADE STUDENT

Eighth-grade students feel like "kings and queens for a day." As one eighth-grade girl expressed it, "We're at the top this year, but next year as freshmen in high school we'll be back at the very bottom. It's a vicious circle." Eighth-grade students display a certain amount of bravado, in spite of the fact that they may not feel as self-assured as they pretend to be. To help them develop a positive self-image, they need many experiences with success. The peer group sets the standard for behavior. Most eighth-grade students are very social minded. They enjoy activities with peers of both sexes. Some eighth-grade students are accomplished musicians, artists, and photographers. A number of eighth-grade students excel in sports. Intramural sports programs are popular with eighth-grade students. Intellectual development is highly variable, but many eighth-grade students are capable of carrying out formal operations, logical reasoning, problem solving, and independent study projects. Continuous progress is the goal for skill development.

Eighth-grade students especially enjoy reading science fiction, fantasy, history, sports stories, adventure, realistic fiction, special interest nonfiction, and love stories. They often complain that the books in the library media center are not mature enough for them. Providing a large collection of paperback books helps to meet some of their needs and desires.

Library media skills lessons for eighth-grade students should provide opportunities for students to develop competencies in reading, writing, speaking, and creative expression. Emphasis should be placed on career development, consumer education, computer literacy, health, foreign language skills, and research skills.

Library media specialists who recognize and understand the characteristics of middle school students are better prepared to provide learning experiences that are relevant to the students' needs.

NOTES

[1] Edward Brazee, "What Are Middle Schools Good For?" *Instructor* 94 (November/December 1982): 31-32.

[2] Conrad F. Toepfer, Jr., "Brain Growth Periodization: A New Dogma for Education," *Middle School Journal* 6 (August 1979): 18-20.

[3] Board of Education of Howard County, Maryland, *The Middle Schools of Howard County: Report of the Citizens' Ad Hoc Committee to Study the Middle Schools* (Ellicott City, Md.: The Board of Education, 1978): 46-57.

BIBLIOGRAPHY

Board of Education of Howard County, Maryland. *The Middle Schools of Howard County: Report of the Citizens' Ad Hoc Committee to Study the Middle Schools.* Ellicott City, Md.: The Board of Education, 1978.

Brazee, Edward. "What Are Middle Schools Good For?" *Instructor* 92 (November/December 1982): 31-33.

Brown, Faith. *Five "R's" for Middle School.* Fairborn, Ohio: National Middle School Association, 1980.

Erb, Thomas O., ed. *Middle School Research Studies, 1981.* Fairborn, Ohio: National Middle School Association, 1981.

Profile of a Middle School. Alexandria, Va.: Association for Supervision and Curriculum Development, 1979. Film.

Toepfer, Conrad F., Jr. "Brain Growth Periodization: A New Dogma for Education." *Middle School Journal* 6 (August 1979): 18-20.

3

Integrated Library Media Skills

INTRODUCTION

The process of planning and designing an integrated library media skills program requires a commitment from the library media specialist and the teacher. To begin an integrated library media skills program, it is advisable for the library media specialist to work with one teacher and to expand the program at designated intervals to include a team, a discipline, and a grade level. As lessons and units are taught and revised, they become the models for additional lessons.

SCOPE AND SEQUENCE

A comprehensive and systematic approach to library media skills instruction must start with the development of objectives for students that will enable them to acquire the necessary skills to become independent learners. The objectives become the basis for scope and sequence statements that are the framework for teaching specific library media skills at each grade level. Presently, many school districts are designing and using scope and sequence charts to enhance the teaching of library media skills.

The library media specialist and teachers can use the scope and sequence statements of library media skills objectives to plan and implement an integrated library media skills program. The library media skills will be taught jointly by the library media specialist and the teacher in the context of the curriculum.

A detailed explanation of the role of the library media specialist and the role of the teacher, as well as a model for integrating library media skills objectives, are given in the following chapters. Examples of integrated lessons and units are given in Part II.

The chart labeled Library Media Skills Objectives: Scope and Sequence (see pages 16-18) is a set of objectives that evolved from the experience of teaching library media skills in middle schools. Each school or school district should determine the scope and sequence of objectives that will meet curricula objectives.

There are five general categories that constitute the library media skills objectives:

1. Orientation and organization
    a. identification of library media personnel, materials, and equipment
    b. location and arrangement of materials and equipment

2. Selection
    a. discrimination of selection appropriate to needs
    b. discrimination of selection of types of media

3. Utilization
    a. identification of concepts
    b. organization and interpretation of data
    c. development of research skills

4. Production
    a. communication of ideas
    b. utilization of skills
    c. presentation in many formats

5. Reading and literature guidance
    a. identification of genres
    b. functional reading strategies
    c. leisure-time activity

The scope and sequence of the library media skills objectives is organized into a combined program of objectives for grades six, seven, and eight. Since the objectives overlap grade levels it is difficult to give specific objectives for each grade level; however, some objectives are stressed more often at a given level. In Part II, which contains examples of lessons for each grade level, there is a brief overview of the objectives for each grade level.

The development of a scope and sequence of library media skills objectives and the integration of these objectives by the library media specialist and the teacher into lessons or units of instruction will establish a basis for an integrated library media skills program.

(Text continues on page 19.)

Library Media Skills Objectives:
Scope and Sequence for Middle School Students

Orientation and Organization

The student will:

1. Identify

    Library media center personnel
    Library media center rules and
        regulations
    Services provided by library media
        center staff
    Procedures to check out and return
        materials
    Classification systems

2. Identify and locate

    Card catalog
    Vertical file
    Reference collection
    Special collections
    Indexes
    Print material
        Books: fiction and nonfiction
        Magazines
        Newspapers
    Nonprint material:
        Films
        Filmstrips
        Filmloops
        Records
        Slides
        Kits
        Charts
        Cassettes
        Transparencies
        Microforms
        Software
        Videotapes
    Equipment:
        Projectors:
            16-mm
            8-mm (Super)
            filmstrip
            opaque
            overhead
            slide
            microform
        Cassette recorder
        Microform reader

Equipment (cont'd.)
    Video recorder
    Record player
    Computer

3. Arrange

    Material based on a specific system
    Alphabetically by author's full name
    Alphabetically by title

4. Locate

    Materials using call numbers
    Specific information using visual and
        audio materials
    Information using bibliographies
    Locate and interpret copyright symbol

Selection

The student will:

1. Select

    Reading as a means of acquiring
        information
    Many types of books according to
        reading level and interests
    Appropriate material for a given purpose
    Print and nonprint material based on
        specific criteria
    Sources based upon authority, accuracy,
        and appropriateness
    Appropriate medium for presentation

2. Select and match equipment with
    material

    16-mm projector—Film
    8-mm projector—Filmloop
    Opaque projector—Opaque materials
    Overhead projector—Transparencies
    Slide projector—Slides
    Microform projector—Microfilm,
        microfiche
    Video recorder—Video cassettes or
        tapes
    Cassette recorder—Cassettes
    Record player—Records
    Computer—Software, diskettes
    Camera—Film for prints or slides

Selection (cont'd.)

3. Select and distinguish

    Between:

    types of indexes
    types of dictionaries
    parts of a book
    types of bibliographies
    purpose and content of encyclopedias
    medium and message

    Among:

    general reference books
    volumes of an encyclopedia
    periodicals for current information
    relevant topics in an index
    similarities and differences of newspapers
    computer programs
    nonprint materials for a given purpose

Utilization

The student will:

1. Identify

    Main idea
    Point of view
    Parts of a book
    Unsubstantiated statements or facts
    Primary and secondary sources
    Audio sequence of events
    Visual sequence of events
    Order:
    alphabetical
    calendar
    chronological
    geographical
    numerical

2. Interpret

    Maps, graphs, charts
    Specialized reference materials to develop and support research
    Information from several sources
    Data bearing on a specific question

3. Locate

    Specific information on a filmstrip or filmloop
    Topics and subtopics using an index
    Illustrations

4. Use

    Information from many sources
    Dewey Decimal System to locate material
    Card catalog using author, title, and subject headings
    Call numbers to locate material
    General reference books:
    Encyclopedias
    Dictionaries
    Atlases
    Handbooks
    Almanacs
    Indexes
    Directories
    Specified reference materials to develop and support research
    Guide words
    Cross references
    Nonprint resources
    Special dictionaries:
    biographical
    geographical
    foreign language
    subject area
    Vertical file
    Resources to organize and prepare a written report
    Organizational skills:
    Outlining
    Notetaking
    Summarizing
    Research skills:
    Skimming to find relevant ideas
    Defining a problem for research
    Drawing appropriate conclusions
    Gaining information from nonfiction
    Paraphrasing or summarizing
    Inferring facts from maps and charts
    Preparing a summary
    Preparing a bibliography
    Observing copyright laws

Production

The student will:

1. Select

   Media format to communicate content
      or ideas
   Appropriate supplies for productions:
      photographic
      drymount and laminating
      art and graphic
      audio
      videotape
      transparency
   Appropriate audiovisual equipment for
      selected presentation

2. Plan media production steps:

   Determining and stating objective
   Determining procedures for chosen media
      format

3. Develop media production that

   Expresses a mood or feeling
   Is based on information from resources

4. Utilize skills

   Organizational
   Artistic
   Creative

5. Produce

   Videotape
   Super 8-mm movie
   Slide/tape
   Photographs
   Multimedia production
   Recording
   Charts
   Displays
   Booklets

6. Evaluate production

Reading and Literature Guidance

The student will:

1. Identify

   Elements of a novel:
      Plot
      Characters
      Setting
   Components of a newspaper
   Characteristics of myths, fables, fairy
      tales, folktales, tall tales, and
      legends
   Content of biographies and auto-
      biographies
   Poetic forms
   Elements of drama
   Types of realistic and nonrealistic
      fiction

2. Develop functional reading strategies

   Locate references
   Follow directions
   Interpret information

3. Select

   Reading as a leisure time activity
   Listening and viewing as a leisure-time
      activity

PROFESSIONAL RESOURCES

Professional resources for teaching library media skills can be used by the library media specialist and the teacher as an aid in planning integrated library media skills lessons. Some recommended sources are included in the bibliography of this chapter.

BIBLIOGRAPHY

Bee, Clifford P. *Secondary Learning Centers: An Innovative Approach to Individualized Instruction.* Santa Monica, Calif.: Goodyear Publishing Company, 1980.

Board of Education of Anne Arundel County, Maryland. *Library Media Skills Scope and Sequence.* Parole, Md.: The Board of Education, 1983.

Board of Education of Montgomery County, Maryland. *Instructional Objectives for Information Retrieval and Media Production.* Rockville, Md.: The Board of Education, 1978.

Board of Education of Washington County, Maryland. *Scope and Sequence of Skills Grades K-12.* Hagerstown, Md.: The Board of Education, 1982.

Carlsen, G. Robert. *Books and the Teen-Age Reader.* New York: Harper & Row, 1971.

Costa, Betty, and Marie Costa. *A Micro Handbook for Small Libraries and Media Centers.* Littleton, Colo.: Libraries Unlimited, Inc., 1983.

Fader, Daniel. *The New Hooked on Books.* New York: Berkley Books, 1976.

Hart, Thomas L. *Instruction in School Media Center Use.* Chicago: American Library Association, 1978.

Howard County Public Schools. *A Curriculum Guide in Library and Media Skills, K-12.* Ellicott City, Md.: Howard County Public School System, 1978.

Katz, William. *Your Library: A Reference Guide.* New York: Holt, Rinehart, and Winston, 1979.

Kemp, Jerrold E. *Planning and Producing Audiovisual Materials.* 4th ed. New York: Harper & Row, 1980.

Margrabe, Mary. *The Now Library.* Washington, D.C.: Acropolis Books, 1973.

Polette, Nancy, and Marjorie Hamlin. *Exploring Books with Gifted Children.* Littleton, Colo.: Libraries Unlimited, Inc., 1980.

Teaching Tips from Kodak. Rochester, N.Y.: Eastman Kodak Company, 1979.

Thomas, James L., and Ruth M. Loring, eds. *Motivating Children and Young Adults to Read.* Phoenix, Ariz.: The Oryx Press, 1979.

Wieckert, Jeanne E., and Irene W. Bell. *Media/Classroom Skills: Games for the Middle School.* 2 vols. Littleton, Colo.: Libraries Unlimited, Inc., 1981.

Wynar, Christine. *Guide to Reference Books for School Media Centers.* 2d ed. Littleton, Colo.: Libraries Unlimited, Inc., 1981.

4

The Role of the Library Media Specialist

The role of the library media specialist is changing in keeping with the changing concepts in education fostered by the information explosion and advances in high technology. The library media specialist plays an important part in helping students learn the skills they will need to function in the current and future technological environment. As a teacher, a provider of services and materials, a resource person, a planner, an innovator of instructional technologies, and a curriculum designer, the library media specialist is directly involved in the learning process.

LEADERSHIP

By accepting the responsibility for the instructional planning and implementation of an integrated library media skills program, the library media specialist provides a key leadership function. The desirable qualities of a good leader include excellent organization, dedication, mutual respect, cooperativeness, consistent behavior, flexible practices, sense of fairness, and good communications. To provide this leadership, the library media specialist should have a thorough knowledge of the structure and purpose of the educational system, the curriculum concepts, the learning abilities and needs of students, and the strengths and capabilities of staff members.

The library media specialist should prepare for this role by a continuing educational program, membership in professional organizations, attending seminars and conventions, and participating in in-service programs. Reading professional journals as well as books for middle school students should have a high priority. The library media specialist should also participate in school activities such as parties, dramas, field trips, outdoor education, recitals, and festivals. Students and teachers respond favorably to the library media specialist's dressing in costumes, telling folktales, and square dancing. Reading curriculum guides and serving on curriculum committees prepares the library media specialist for work with team leaders and individual teachers in coordinating the teaching of library media skills with the curriculum.

MOTIVATION

Motivation is a key ingredient for the library media specialist and the teacher in the implementation of an integrated library media skills program. There are several motivating factors that should influence the library media specialist toward an active participation in the instructional process. They include (1) the opportunity to contribute toward the students' intellectual, social, and emotional growth, (2) the desire to provide services to the users of the library media center,

(3) the encouragement to create new programs, (4) the utilization of training in instructional methods, (5) the improvement of effectiveness, (6) the planning for optimal use of resources, (7) the challenge of new technology, (8) the demands for accountability, (9) the involvement in curriculum planning, and (10) the participation in activities throughout the school.

The library media specialist can be a motivating force to help teachers accept and participate in the integration of a library media skills program into curriculum. Some suggestions are:

1. Get to know teachers.

2. Show empathy and concern.

3. Invite teachers to open houses, to celebrations, and to in-service programs.

4. Provide refreshments.

5. Remember birthdays and special occasions with a bookmark, a special card, or a chocolate chip cookie.

6. Provide a comfortable, attractive, professional resources area.

7. Route professional journals to subject area teachers.

8. Prepare guidelines: *What the Library Media Center Can Do for You and What You Can Do for the Library Media Center.*

9. Provide lists of library media skills objectives.

10. Be available for planning.

11. Attend team planning sessions.

12. Set up a yearly planning calendar.

13. Invite teachers to schedule a planning time.

14. Share ideas.

15. Consult with teachers.

16. Jointly plan performance objectives.

17. Share responsibility for teaching.

18. Offer to work with small groups or individuals.

19. Suggest ideas for student productions.

20. Provide a bibliography of print and nonprint resources.

21. Assist with locating information through public library, colleges or universities, or community resources.

22. Help set up learning centers and displays.

23. Offer to go to team or class area for large group or small group presentations.

24. Read, correct, and grade part of students' work.

25. Jointly evaluate lessons or units.

26. Provide feedback.

27. Ask teachers to preview materials.

28. Purchase materials suggested by teachers, in accordance with selection policies.

29. Provide a variety of services.

30. Cooperate with all staff members.

GOALS

The goals for an integrated library media skills program at an individual school are based on the goals developed for the library media program by the school system. These goals can be adapted to meet the needs of that school and community through the combined efforts of the library media specialist, the principal, and the teachers. Inherent in these goals is the responsibility to develop independent learners by teaching students the skills of locating, analyzing, interpreting, producing, and utilizing all forms of media. Students should be encouraged to seek out and discover new ideas, to explore new concepts, to ask questions, to make choices and decisions, to solve problems, and to modify and change answers. The goals of providing students with meaningful, relevant, and challenging materials correlates with the integration of library media skills with curriculum. Additional goals include providing an environment where students will (1) develop freedom for self-selection, evaluation, and the discriminate use of information sources, (2) grow in reading ability, interests, and choices, (3) strive for excellence, (4) develop a commitment to their own education and a responsibility for their choices, and (5) learn to make realistic choices for the future.

COOPERATIVE PLANNING

Cooperative planning with the principal, supervisors, teachers, students, and parents is essential for the achievement of a successful library media skills program integrated with the curriculum.

Joint planning by the library media specialist and teachers provides the structure and support for the instructional design of an integrated library media skills program. Planning of the program is discussed in greater detail with examples in chapter 5, "The Role of the Teacher."

PRINCIPAL

The library media specialist must schedule planning sessions with the principal to discuss and evaluate the general goals and objectives and desired learning outcomes of the program. The outcome of one planning session where the library media specialist expressed to the principal the need for more involvement with the computer program resulted in the establishment of a committee composed of the math team, team leaders, the library media specialist, and the principal. The committee defined the objectives for computer usage, surveyed the facilities for allocation of space, recommended the establishment of a computer center in the library media center, prepared a proposal for budgetary support, established criteria for the review and evaluation of software, drew up guidelines for use of the center by teachers and students, and defined responsibilities. The library media specialist became directly involved with teachers in planning lessons and units associated with computers. The principal provided the administrative support for the program.

By providing joint planning time and encouraging teachers to plan and share teaching responsibilities with the library media specialist, the principal can promote an integrated library media skills program. Active support should include allocation of funds for resources, overseeing the implementation of policies and procedures, and participation in promotional activities. By observing, analyzing, and evaluating a lesson or unit jointly taught by the library media specialist and a teacher, the principal can identify needs, facilitate communication and cooperation, appraise effectiveness, and provide motivation for improving the effectiveness of the program.

The library media specialist can inform the principal about successful programs, problems, needs, and activities in the library media center. The principal can be invited to observe and participate in games, projects, fairs, news quiz programs, and productions. The importance of the support and guidance of the principal in implementing, strengthening, and evaluating a unified library media skills program cannot be overestimated.

SUPERVISORS

At the school system level, the supervisors provide the impetus for the planning and development of an integrated library media program. The supervisor of library media services, in accordance with school board procedures, generates the policies, goals, and objectives that provide the framework for the program. A curriculum guide containing library media skills objectives and recommendations for their integration into specific curriculum areas will greatly facilitate the implementation of the program. The supervisor of library media services should work with subject supervisors to plan strategies for the cooperative teaching of library media skills. Support for the program in each library media center by the library media supervisor is an ongoing process providing in-service training, feedback and interaction, and encouragement.

Getting to know the subject supervisors by name and talking with them when they visit in school will help to establish a foundation for support of an integrated library media skills program. When the subject supervisor observes an integrated library media skills lesson being taught by the subject area teacher and the library media specialist, the supervisor can be asked for comments and suggestions. Additional ideas on the teaching of library media skills, the use of the library media center, the recommendations for purchase of resources by the library media specialist can be solicited from the subject supervisor. They can also be asked to include a library media specialist in curriculum workshops and in-service meetings to provide input for the integration of library media skills into classroom instructional units and curriculum guides.

STUDENTS

Students can be included in the planning process through class discussions, individual conferences, and lesson or unit evaluations. If students are a part of an independent study program, they will meet regularly with their advisor and the library media specialist to plan strategies, to review and evaluate progress, to judge the adequacy of resources, and to receive guidance. Two students who would like to work on an independent project for science class, for example, could write a proposal for researching and explaining the theory of platetectonics and present it to the science teacher. The library media specialist can become a part of the planning team along with the science teacher and students. Together they can meet to plan the objectives, assign the responsibilities, design the project, determine the schedule, and define the evaluative criteria. The library media specialist can discuss and review selection, location, and utilization skills with the students who meet in the library media center during their independent study time. The students will be expected to successfully utilize the card catalog, encyclopedias, reference books, and indexes to locate print and nonprint resources. Requesting additional resources through the interlibrary loan network can be accomplished by using the microfiche union catalog in the library media center. The students can consult several sources, analyze data while discriminating between relevant and irrelevant facts, summarize and draw conclusions, and prepare an outline to submit to the science teacher. After obtaining suggestions and approval from the science teacher, the students can write a report and consult with the library media specialist concerning the format for making a bibliography. The students can then apply their researched information by planning and producing a super 8-mm movie with the assistance of the library media specialist. The science teacher and library media specialist would jointly evaluate and critique the project.

Middle school students enjoy helping plan activities, and it is important to include their input when planning media-related field trips, celebrations, festivals, and productions. When activities in the library media center include small group participation, students can be allowed to plan alternative methods to reach the objective. Joint planning with the teachers, the library media specialist, and students is very important for the creation and production of audiovisual programs. If the industrial arts teacher wants three students to plan and produce single concept films demonstrating safety procedures when using machines, the industrial arts teacher can meet with the library media specialist, explain the objectives, and plan the schedule. The library media specialist can work with the students and assist them in planning a storyboard, preparing visuals, filming, editing, and evaluating. The library media specialist would serve as a resource person and technical advisor. One of the goals of a library media specialist is developing the ability to cooperatively plan with students.

PARENTS

Communication is the key to cooperative planning between the library media specialist and parents. By informing parents of the general goals and objectives of the library media skills program, the library media specialist activates the communications process. An orientation meeting for the parents of incoming sixth-grade students, a library media center open house during the PTA Back-to-School Night, a survey of service needs, an invitation to schedule a visit during parent/teacher conference periods, and a library media center newsletter sent to parents are some suggested activities to gain the interest and support of parents.

Parent volunteers in the library media center provide assistance to the library media specialist by performing clerical duties, helping with book fairs, assisting with audiovisual productions, and participating in field trips. An explanation of the goals and objectives of the library media program is included in the training session for volunteers. These parents may become members of a library media center advisory committee. Because of their firsthand experience in the library media center, they become strong advocates in support of the budget, the acquisition policies, and the overall library media program.

PROCEDURES

The formulation of procedures that facilitate the integration of library media skills with the curriculum is a function of the administrative, service, and instructional roles of the library media specialist.

A quality library media program must be built on a foundation of effective administrative procedures. The efficient daily management of library media center routines necessitates well-defined operations for the circulation of media materials and equipment, scheduling of classes and productions, orderly conduct of business, and organization of resources. Budgeting, evaluation and selection of materials, inventory, and maintenance are necessary functions that must be carefully performed. The library media specialist needs to prepare a flexible monthly schedule for administrative tasks. An example of such a monthly schedule follows.

The service role of the library media specialist includes a wide range of reference, bibliographic, and production services to teachers and students. The extent of these services should be determined by establishing service preferences and priorities. James W. Liesener, in his book *A Systematic Process for Planning Media Programs*, provides the process and techniques for the development of a responsive and effective program of library media services in terms of functions performed for the client.[1]

With the strong emphasis on the involvement of the library media specialist in the instructional program, the instructional role of the library media specialist should include formal and informal teaching, in-service training, and reading guidance. As a teacher, the library media specialist should prepare general instructional objectives and specific performance objectives for units and lessons. Using a variety of teaching strategies and instructional materials, emphasis should be placed on skill

SEPTEMBER 1983

ADMINISTRATIVE TASKS

SUNDAY	MONDAY	TUESDAY	WEDNESDAY	THURSDAY	FRIDAY	SATURDAY
				1 Put up displays / Arrange reading area / Bring in plants	**2** Assign and deliver equipment / Prepare notices for faculty meeting	**3** Write long-range goals and yearly objectives
4	**5** HOLIDAY LABOR DAY	**6** Check in magazines / File catalogs / Order newspapers / Send school schedule	**7** *Plan budget!* / Print / Nonprint / Supplies / Expendable materials	**8** Type budget / Make appointment with principal / Give out applications for student assistants / ROSH HASHANAH	**9** Meet with principal to discuss budget and objectives / Take home journals / Plan schedule	**10** Read reviews for selection of print and nonprint materials
11	**12** Order supplies / Promote interlibrary loan	**13** Write notice for PTA newsletter asking for parent volunteers	**14** Publish ITV schedule / Order film	**15** Order software for preview / File cards in card catalog	**16** Select student assistants / Make weekly assignments / Plan schedule	**17** Visit public library / Read
			INTERVIEW STUDENT ASSISTANTS			
18	**19** Type print and nonprint order	**20** Process new books / Select books to read	**21** Plan open house for faculty: / Displays / Handouts / Refreshments	**22** Meet with Camera Club / Discuss book fair plans with team leaders	**23** Check equipment for maintenance / Prepare capital budget requests / Plan schedule	**24** Read
			TRAIN STUDENT ASSISTANTS			
25	**26** Read new curriculum guides / Weed vertical file	**27** Plan displays for October / Train parent volunteers	**28** Set up and hold open house for faculty after school	**29** Review circulation records	**30** Write overdues / Put up display after school / Plan schedule	

YOM KIPPUR (on the 16/17 weekend row)

development. Large and small group discussions, media presentations, individual and group projects, learning stations, and exploratory activities should promote the students' intellectual and social development. *The Teaching Role of the School Media Specialist* by Kay E. Vandergrift contains many excellent suggestions and provocative ideas.[2] Teaching in-service training programs for student assistants, parent volunteers, and teachers can help to strengthen the library media program. Reading guidance and the appreciation or love of books can be incorporated not only in book talks but also in lessons and units jointly taught by the library media specialist and teachers. For example:

UNIT	BOOKS
Explorers	Heyerdahl, Thor. *Kon Tiki.*
Indians	Kroeber, T. *Ishi, Last of His Tribe.*
Animals	Eckert, A. W. *Incident at Hawk's Hill.*
Careers	Sterling, P. *Sea and Earth: The Life of Rachel Carson.*

It is through direct experiences with books that students can experience discovery, magic, mystery, and sheer delight. The library media specialist working with middle school students has a great opportunity to share the joy of reading and to turn students on to the exciting, challenging world of books.

SELECTION AND UTILIZATION OF RESOURCES

The selection and utilization of materials and equipment to support the instructional program is a major responsibility of the library media specialist. The library media specialist can use a variety of selection aids based on the school system's selection policy. By using the established criteria for the evaluation of instructional materials, the library media specialist and teachers can preview and evaluate many materials that meet the learning needs of students. The library media center collection should provide a broad range of materials with a vertical and horizontal continuum of subject matter that supports the students' inquiry process, concept formation, and intellectual and emotional growth.

Meaningful classification and organization of all materials will extend the usefulness of the collection. A yearly inventory with emphasis on weeding and replacement will greatly enhance the collection.

Students, teachers, and administrators must be invited and welcomed to the library media center. Every effort must be made to facilitate the use of all the resources. The library media specialist should establish flexible guidelines for the loan of books, materials, and equipment. An up-to-date, well-organized collection that is easily accessible and available is the key to successful utilization.

Curriculum design and implementation is the area in which the library media specialist has the greatest latitude for creative expression.[3] It is essential that the library media specialist be knowledgeable about the schoolwide curriculum, and this knowledge can serve as a framework for writing, developing, and implementing library media skills into all areas of the curriculum. By reading curriculum guides, observing classroom instruction, and discussing needs with teachers and supervisors, the library media specialist can discover many possibilities for designing lessons and units to extend, enrich, and supplement the existing curriculum.

The evaluation and assessment of the library media program should be an ongoing process for the library media specialist. From the evaluation and selection of resources and equipment, the review of the collection, the assessment of services, to the teaching and evaluation of lessons and units, the procedures for assessment should be built into the prescribed activity through well-defined objectives. The standard of performance set by the objectives becomes a measure of accountability. Using the data formulated from assessments, the library media specialist can revise, restructure, and improve many aspects of the library media program.

NOTES

[1] James W. Liesener, *A Systematic Process for Planning Media Programs* (Chicago: American Library Association, 1976), 1-8, 30-42.

[2] Kay E. Vandergrift, *The Teaching Role of the School Media Specialist* (Chicago: American Library Association, 1979), 18-30.

[3] David Loertscher, "The Second Revolution: A Taxonomy for the 1980's," *Wilson Library Bulletin* 56 (February, 1982): 417-21.

BIBLIOGRAPHY

Barry, Ann. "Winning Public Support for the School Library." *The Book Report* 1 (September/October 1982): 48-49.

Blazek, Ron. *Influencing Students toward Media Center Use.* Chicago: American Library Association, 1975.

Chisholm, Margaret E., and Donald P. Ely. *Instructional Design and the Library Media Specialist.* Chicago: American Library Association, 1979.

Davies, Ruth Ann. *The School Library Center: A Force for Educational Excellence.* New York: Bowker, 1974.

Glasser, William. *Schools without Failure.* New York: Harper & Row, 1969.

Liesener, James W. *A Systematic Process for Planning Media Programs.* Chicago: American Library Association, 1976.

Loertscher, David. "The Second Revolution: A Taxonomy for the 1980's." *Wilson Library Bulletin* 56 (February 1982): 417-21.

Rossoff, Martin. *The School Library and Educational Change.* Littleton, Colo.: Libraries Unlimited, Inc., 1971.

Salle, Ellen M. "Riding the Wave of the Future: Media Specialists Face a New Age." *School Library Journal* 29 (March 1983): 126.

Vandergrift, Kay E. *The Teaching Role of the School Media Specialist.* Chicago: American Library Association, 1979.

Wehmeyer, Lillian B. *The School Librarian as Educator.* Littleton, Colo.: Libraries Unlimited, Inc., 1976.

Wilson, Pauline. "Librarians as Teachers." *Library Quarterly* 49 (April 1979): 146-62.

5

The Role
of the Teacher

The role of the teacher in a middle school is characterized by the level of the teacher's commitment to the philosophy of middle schools. An effective middle school teacher recognizes the unique physical, social, emotional, and intellectual needs of students and uses a variety of techniques to meet these needs. The development of the skills of reading, writing, listening, and computation is practiced in the context of content areas. The processes of reasoning, problem solving, interpreting, applying, analyzing, and evaluating become goals for student attainment based on the student's ability. Using the levels of student achievement, the teacher plans a continuous progress program to provide appropriate instruction in many subject areas. Special attention is given to fostering a positive self-image in each student. All of these factors influence the cooperative effort of the teacher and the library media specialist in designing and implementing a library media skills program that is an integral part of the instruction program.

INTEGRATION OF OBJECTIVES

Before effective and meaningful planning for an integrated library media skills program can take place, the teacher and library media specialist must thoroughly comprehend and interpret the scope and sequence of library media skills objectives as well as the curriculum objectives for the subject. The list of library media skills objectives can be more readily incorporated into the yearly curriculum plans when the teacher and library media specialist share and analyze the list together.

Library media skills can be integrated into a teaching unit by merging the instructional objectives and the library media skills objectives into one set of unit objectives and precise performance objectives. An integrated model for library media skills instruction presented in *Teaching Library Media Skills* by H. Thomas Walker and Paula Kay Montgomery illustrates the process of combining objectives into a single instructional unit taught jointly by the teacher and library media specialist.[1]

Integrated Model of Library Media Skills Instruction

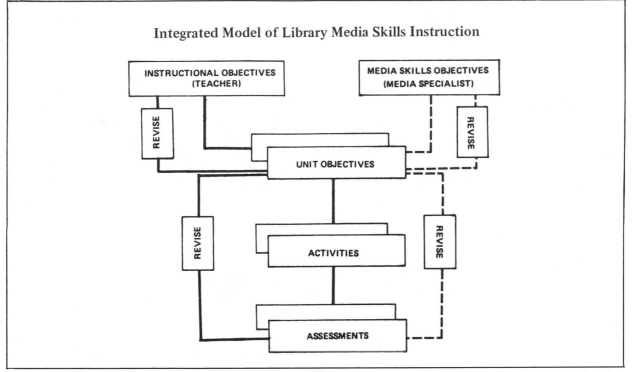

Reprinted, by permission, from H. Thomas Walker and Paula Kay Montgomery, *Teaching Library Media Skills,* 2d ed. (Littleton, Colo.: Libraries Unlimited, Inc., 1983).

The teacher and library media specialist must invest a great deal of time and effort in jointly planning teaching units and lessons. The methods of planning may vary according to the needs, circumstances, schedules, and styles of the teacher and the library media specialist. Planning may begin when

- a science teacher schedules a planning time with the library media specialist to discuss the science fair.

- the library media specialist shares an idea with the reading teacher.

- an art teacher asks for help with an animated movie.

- a language arts teacher asks the library media specialist to recommend literary works for intensive study.

- the library media specialist invites the math teachers for afternoon coffee to discuss the computer program.

- a social studies teacher asks the library media specialist to obtain resources for a unit on taxes.

- a music teacher requests the use of the library media center for learning centers on musical theater.

- a science teacher sends a note asking if it would be convenient to use the video equipment the following week for closed circuit viewing of a bug race.

- a physical education teacher comments in the lunchroom that it has been difficult to plan a theme for the gymnastic show and asks the library media specialist for ideas.

- the library media specialist wants to have a celebration during National Library Week.

These types of experiences provide the stimulus for the joint planning and teaching of integrated library media skills lessons and units.

The planning process for the teacher and library media specialist should include

1. Discussion of tentative plans, concepts, and generalizations.

2. Outline of content.

3. Resources.

4. Suggested procedures.

5. Schedules.

6. Instructional objectives of teacher.

7. Library media skills objectives.

8. Integrated lesson or unit objectives.

9. Performance objectives.

10. Duties and responsibilities of teacher.

11. Duties and responsibilities of library media specialist.

12. Learning activities.

13. Initiation of lesson.

14. Grouping.

15. Culminating activities.

16. Evaluation.

The following example illustrates the process and planning of a unit entitled "The Play's the Thing." The library media specialist received a note from a language arts teacher stating the desire to plan research activities on Shakespeare, Elizabethan England, the Globe Theatre, and *Twelfth Night* beginning on November 10. The library media specialist went to the teacher's planning area during planning time and discussed tentative plans. After collecting resources from the school library media center, the public library, and from interlibrary loan, the library media specialist invited the teacher to the library media center after school to review resources, prepare an outline, determine objectives, and assign responsibilities. The teacher wanted to familiarize the students with the history and background of Elizabethan England and to arouse student interest in reading *Twelfth Night*. The unit would include a field trip to attend a university production of *Twelfth Night*. The culminating activity would be the presentation of oral reports or projects by students. Helping to plan the activities provided the opportunity for the library media specialist to incorporate many library media skills.

Title: The Play's the Thing.

Language Arts Instructional Objectives:

Examine and interpret political, social, and literary life and customs of the period.

Read the play.

Analyze basic plot structure.

Select passages that reveal conflicts.

Identify the theme.

Identify and list the main characters.

List the sequence of events.

Analyze outcome.

Prepare oral report or project.

Library Media Skills Objectives:

Use the card catalog to locate material or information.

Use an index.

Use special dictionaries.

Interpret information found in resources.

Identify form or genre, theme, and point of view.

Produce a media presentation that contains specific subject matter.

Unit Objectives (Integrated):

Examine and interpret political, social, and literary life and customs of the period.

Use the card catalog to locate material or information.

Use subject-oriented resources.

Interpret information found in resources.

Identify genre.

Read the play.

Analyze basic plot structure.

Identify the theme.

Identify and list the main characters.

Select passages that reveal conflicts.

List sequence of events.

Analyze outcome.

Prepare an oral report, project, or media production.

Performance Objective: Given lectures and audiovisual presentations on Elizabethan England and William Shakespeare and a review of reference sources; the students will complete a reference assignment; read, view, and analyze the play *Twelfth Night*, and prepare an oral report or project.

The teacher will:

1. Introduce the unit and explain the objectives.
2. Ask the library media specialist to give a lecture on the life of William Shakespeare.
3. Assign topics for research.
4. Schedule classes in the library media center.
5. Use teachers' guide to *Twelfth Night* from the BBC-TV and Time-Life Television Public Broadcasting Service. (Includes poster, recording, discussion questions, record guide handout, viewing guide with synopsis, and teachers' guide.)
6. Have students read and discuss the play before viewing.
7. Plan for the students to view the play on television, film, or as a live production at a theater.
8. Prepare questions for discussion based on unit objectives.
9. Schedule showing of student projects and oral presentations.
10. Evaluate student activities and projects with the library media specialist.

The library media specialist will:

1. Present an audiovisual presentation on the life of William Shakespeare.
2. Review reference sources with students:
   Subject headings:
   > England.
   > William Shakespeare.
   > English Literature.
   > Drama.
   > Theater.
   > Elizabethan Age.

   Reference books:
   > *Oxford Companion to English Literature.*
   > *World Drama.*
   > *New Century Cyclopedia of Names.*
   > *Bartlett's Familiar Quotations.*
   > *Asimov's Guide to Shakespeare.*
3. Obtain resource materials for teacher.
4. Read and study play for background knowledge.
5. View play with class (preferably as a field trip to see a live production).
6. Assist students with projects: slide/tape, posters, models, video tape.
7. Evaluate student activities and unit with teacher.

The student will:

1. Discuss life of William Shakespeare after presentation by library media specialist.
2. Sign up and complete research on one of the following topics:
   William Shakespeare, the Man and Playwright.

   1._____   3._____

   2._____   4._____

Queen Elizabeth I and Her Reign.

1. _____   3. _____

2. _____   4. _____

Shakespeare's England (Life and Culture).

1. _____   3. _____

2. _____   4. _____

The Globe and Other Elizabethan Theaters.

1. _____   3. _____

2. _____   4. _____

Costumes of Shakespeare's Theater.

1. _____   3. _____

2. _____   4. _____

Facts and Anecdotes about the Plays, Poems, and Sonnets.

1. _____   3. _____

2. _____   4. _____

Stratford-upon-Avon, Then and Now.

1. _____   3. _____

2. _____   4. _____

3. Read and discuss the play *Twelfth Night.*
4. View and analyze the play using the following study guide:

Twelfth Night

Setting—give time and place.
Plot—list beginning, middle, ending.
Main Characters—name and describe.
Sequence of events—list.
Passages that reveal conflict—note act, scene, line.
Conclusion—state your reaction.

5. Complete a project or prepare and present an oral report.

Evaluative Criteria: The student will successfully complete a reference assignment; read, view, and analyze the play *Twelfth Night*; and prepare an oral report or project.

The teacher should consider the library media specialist a team member who can provide unique skills to all areas of the curriculum. Cooperative teaching can utilize the strengths of the teacher and the library media specialist as they become partners in instructional design and implementation. Several examples are

- Library media specialist—film making.
  Art teacher—props, set design, titles.

- Health teacher—facts about drugs.
  Library media specialist—resources for reports.

- Language arts teacher—dictionary skills.
  Library media specialist—word search, puzzles.

- Library media specialist—forms of poetry.
  Language arts teacher—photography.

- Math teacher—metric system.
  Library media specialist—metric learning center.

- Library media specialist—listening skills.
  Music teacher—great composers.

- Reading teacher—comprehension and study skills.
  Library media specialist—book talks and promotions.

- Science teacher—concepts and generalizations.
  Library media specialist—outlining and note taking.

- Library media specialist—travelogue to Mexico.
  Social studies teacher—games of Mexico.

- Library media specialist—techniques of debating.
  Social studies teacher—problems, issues, and resources.

SCHEDULING

Careful attention to scheduling is vital for a successful integrated library media skills program. The teacher and library media specialist should chart as many lessons and units as possible on a monthly and weekly calendar. Specific days and periods can be scheduled in the teacher's plan book *and* the library media specialist's plan book. Time allotments should be flexible, but good communications are necessary to ensure the best use of everyone's time. If an entire class is scheduled for a lesson in the library media center, the teacher should accompany the class and participate in the learning activities since joint teaching requires the involvement of both the teacher and the library media specialist. Of course, there will be many times when the library media specialist will work with individuals and groups in the library media center or in other areas of the school while the teacher remains in the classroom with other students. This requires detailed scheduling especially when students are involved in projects and productions. After a timetable has been determined by the teacher and the library media specialist, students should be given a schedule along with the requirements for the unit.

The standards for student behavior should be jointly set by the teacher and library media specialist based on the policies of the school. Maintaining consistent discipline, whether in the classroom or in the library media center, is of the utmost importance in implementing a quality integrated library media skills program.

In the education process, no role is more important than that of the teacher. For it is the teacher who must bridge theory and practice, develop curricula, diagnose and prescribe learning activities, interact with students, and effectively manage and teach students. As competent professionals, teachers must continue to learn new strategies and methodologies gained from research. The library media specialist can provide much needed assistance by sharing some of the teacher's work load. The cooperative venture of planning, designing, and implementing an integrated library media skills program adds the dimension of the expertise of the library media specialist to the instructional program.

NOTES

[1] H. Thomas Walker and Paula Kay Montgomery, *Teaching Library Media Skills,* 2d ed. (Littleton, Colo.: Libraries Unlimited, Inc., 1983), 24.

BIBLIOGRAPHY

Doda, Nancy. *Teacher to Teacher.* Fairborn, Ohio: National Middle School Association, 1981.

Hoover, Kenneth H. *Secondary/Middle School Teaching: A Handbook for Beginning Teachers and Teacher Self-Renewal.* Boston: Allyn and Bacon, 1977.

Joyce, Bruce, and Marsha Weil. *Models of Teaching.* Tarrytown, N.Y.: Prentice-Hall, 1972.

Klingele, W. E. *Teaching in Middle Schools.* Boston: Allyn and Bacon, 1979.

"Librarians and English Teachers: Part II." *English Journal* 70 (November 1981): 75-76.

Schein, Martha P., and Bernard Schein. *Open Classrooms in the Middle School.* West Nyack, N.Y.: Parker Publishing Co., 1975.

Walker, H. Thomas, and Paula Kay Montgomery. *Teaching Library Media Skills.* 2d ed. Littleton, Colo.: Libraries Unlimited, Inc., 1983.

PART II
Library Media Skills
Lessons

Introduction

Part II contains examples of integrated library media skills lessons that are appropriate for middle school students. Selected resources from Part II are given at the end of this part. The principles discussed in Part I—the middle school concept, characteristics of middle school students, and the roles of the library media specialist and teachers—were the basis on which the following sample lessons were developed.

The sample lessons were designed to assist the library media specialist and the teacher in providing a framework for a dynamic library media skills program integrated with the curriculum. The lessons provide ideas and suggestions for a library media skills program for grades six through eight. Careful consideration must be given to the development of lessons based on the guidelines and curricula established by the school system.

Lessons are designated by grade levels, and organized as a continuum for grades six, seven, and eight.

Each lesson contains the following:

Title: Description or slogan.

Overview: Purpose.

Library Media Objectives: Library media skills integrated with content objectives.

Performance Objective: Specific observable behavior and conditions of performance.

Subject area: Department, content area, or discipline.

Learning Strategy: Instructional variables.

Resources: Materials and selected bibliography.

Methods:

> The teacher will: Suggestions and responsibilities for teachers.
>
> The library media specialist will: Suggestions and responsibilities for library media specialists.
>
> The student will: Activities for students.

Evaluative Criteria: Criteria of acceptable student performance.

6 *Skills Lessons for Grade Six*

LESSON 1

Title: Orientation—World of Media.

Overview: The purpose of this lesson is to introduce sixth-grade students to the world of media as an orientation to the library media center. Students will learn about the resources, the personnel, and the policies and procedures of the library media center.

Library Media Skills Objectives:

Identify library media center personnel.

Identify resources.

Performance Objectives: Given a library media center orientation program, the students will be able to name: the library media center personnel, five or more resources, and three or more policies for the use of the library media center.

Subject Area: Language Arts.

Learning Strategy: Large group instruction.

Resources:

Equipment: Overhead projector, cassette recorder, screens, 16-mm projector, super 8-mm projector, record player, filmstrip projector, microfiche projector, television monitor, books, magazines, reference books, newspapers, models, globes, nonprint materials for each piece of equipment.

Kit: *Spiderman.* McGraw-Hill.

Sound Filmstrip: *Dinosaurs.* National Geographic.

8-mm Film loop: *Optical Illusion.* Encyclopaedia Britannica Corp.

Cassette: *The Wizard of Oz.* Camden.

Record: *Wonderfulness: The Amazing Comedy of Bill Cosby.* Warner Brothers.

Videotape: *The Fly.* Perspective.

Microfiche: *Haunted Spacesuit and Other Science Fiction Stories.* American Education Publishers.

Policies and Procedures of the Library Media Center.

Overhead transparencies (see page 42).

(Text continues on page 43.)

Policies and Procedures of the Library Media Center

BORROWING RULES

1. *Two weeks loan:* All fiction and nonfiction books except REFERENCE BOOKS.

2. Books may be renewed.

3. *Overnight Loan:* All reference books including encyclopedias, filmstrips, slides, records, cassettes, kits, games.

   Equipment: Cassette recorders, filmstrip previewers, slide previewers. Special arrangements may be made to borrow additional types of equipment.

4. *Honor checkout system:* Sign your name and homebase to the print, nonprint, or equipment card. Drop card in slot in main desk. Take a date due card. There are no fines but you are expected to return materials on or before the due date.

HOURS

1. One half hour before and after school each day. You may make arrangements with the library media staff for additional hours after school.

2. At lunch. Passes are available each morning before homebase.

3. During entire school day. Individuals and small groups are always welcome. Classes will be scheduled jointly by teachers and the library media specialist.

LIBRARY MEDIA STAFF

Mrs. Van Vliet, Library media specialist.

Mrs. Weller, Library media aide.

Media Techs, student assistants.

Volunteers, parent assistants.

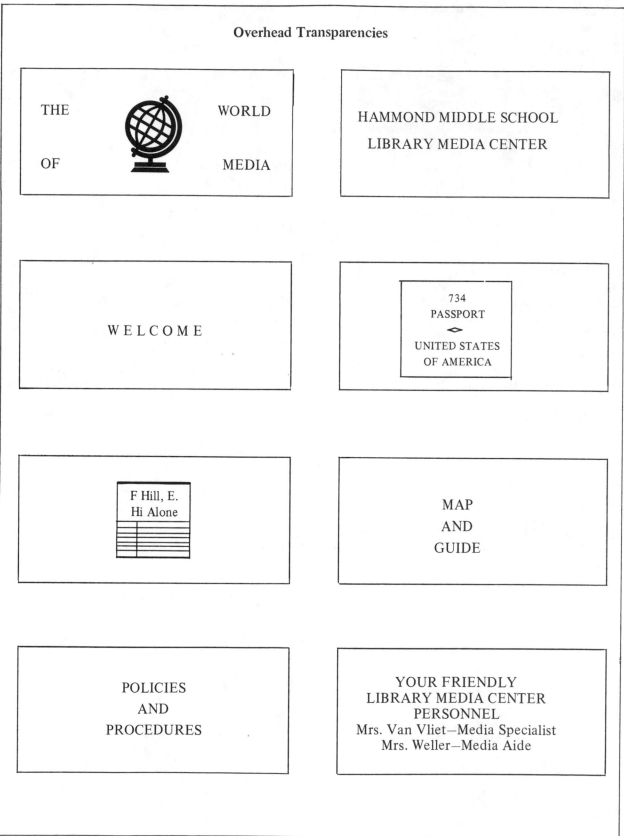

Overhead Transparencies

Methods:

The teacher will:

1.   Schedule the large group instruction by the library media specialist.
2.   Review the lesson with a class discussion the following day.

The library media specialist will:

1.   Prepare transparencies.
2.   Gather resource materials and equipment.
3.   Give large group instruction.

- Set up large group area with overhead projector in the middle. Use transparency "The World of Media."
- Have all equipment with programs running at the same time as students are being seated. Let students be bombarded with the sight and sound for approximately five minutes.
- Change the transparency to the title of library media center. Loudly state "In our library media center we have televisions...record players...16-mm projectors..." Turn off each piece of equipment as it is named. Show books, newspapers, magazines, globes, and models.
- Show the transparency of a passport. State "You need a passport to gain entry into most countries of the world."
- Show transparency of a book card. State "This is your entry into a world of reading. Just sign the cards and leave them at the circulation desk."
- Show transparency of map and guide. State "You will be given a map of the floor plan of the library media center by your social studies teacher tomorrow. You will be taken on a guided tour by the library media center personnel."
- Show transparency with names of the library media center personnel.
- Show transparency of policies and procedures. Give each student a copy of the policies. Read each statement.
- Show transparency "The World of Media" and play the record as students return to class.

The students will:

1.   View multimedia production.
2.   Listen to the library media specialist.
3.   Read the policies and procedures.
4.   Discuss library media center policies and procedures during class.

Evaluative Criteria: The students will correctly name the library media center personnel, five or more resources, and three or more policies of the library media center.

LESSON 2

Title: Puzzled about Your Media Center?

Overview: The purpose of this lesson is to help students define the following terms—main desk, general reference books, card catalog, Dewey Decimal System, nonprint materials, microcat, and vertical file—by completing a puzzle.

Library Media Skills Objectives:

Identify: Card catalog, reference books, Dewey Decimal System, nonprint materials, microcat, vertical file.

Performance Objective: Given a puzzle and a key, the students will correctly solve the puzzle by matching the terms with their meanings.

Subject Area: Language Arts.

Learning Strategy: Puzzle.

Resources:

Key

Puzzle (see page 46).

Methods:

The teacher will:

1. Schedule students to continue the orientation program in the library media center.
2. Check the completed puzzles and answer questions students may ask.

The library media specialist will:

1. Construct 10 keys and puzzles.
2. Cut the keys into jigsaw pieces and put them into envelopes.
3. Divide students into groups of 3 to complete key and puzzle.

The students will:

1. Complete the key and puzzle.
2. Ask the teacher or library media specialist to check the solution.

Evaluative Criteria: The students will correctly solve the library media center puzzle.

(Text continues on page 47.)

Key

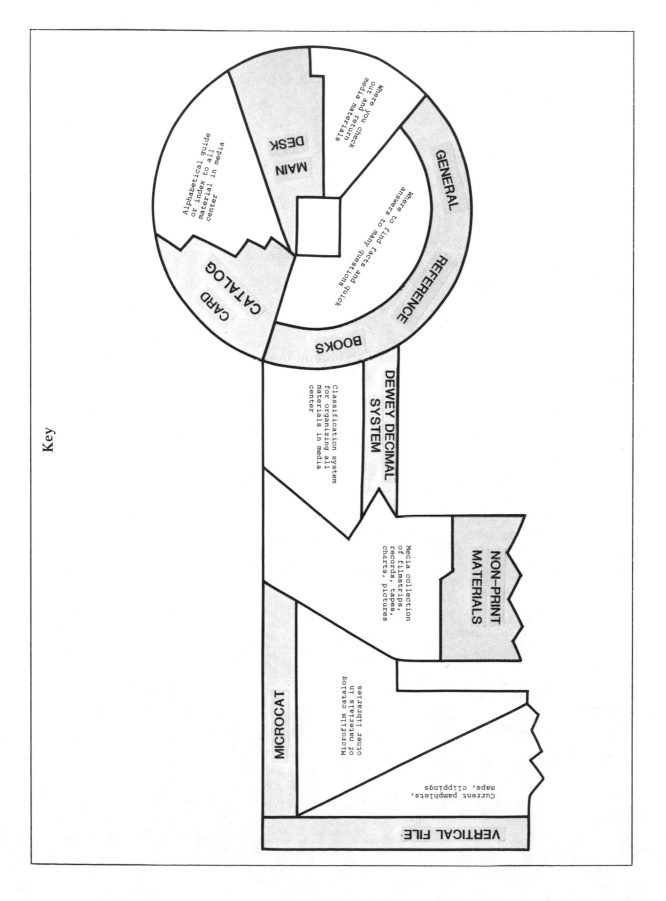

MAIN DESK — Where you check out media and return materials

CARD CATALOG — Alphabetical guide or index to all material in media center

GENERAL REFERENCE BOOKS — Where to find facts and quick answers to many questions

DEWEY DECIMAL SYSTEM — Classification system for organizing all materials in media center

NON-PRINT MATERIALS — Media collection of filmstrips, records, tapes, charts, pictures

MICROCAT — Microfilm catalog of materials in other libraries

VERTICAL FILE — Current pamphlets, maps, clippings

Puzzled about your media center??? Find solutions by completing the puzzle using the key.

Puzzle

Use your completed key to help you write in what the terms listed here mean.

Card Catalog.

Dewey Decimal System.

General Reference Books.

Main Desk.

Microcat.

Nonprint Materials.

Vertical File.

LESSON 3

Title: Following Directions: Mapping Your Way.

Overview: The purpose of this orientation lesson is to help students understand the organization of resources in the library media center by completing a map of the physical location of resources. They will listen attentively and follow directions.

Library Media Skills Objectives:

Locate fiction and nonfiction collections.

Locate card catalog.

Locate the vertical file.

Locate encyclopedias.

Locate magazines.

Locate nonprint materials.

Locate audiovisual equipment.

Performance Objective: Given a map of the library media center, a list of areas, and signs or labels in the areas, the students will complete the map by identifying and labeling the areas on the list.

Subject Area: Social Studies.

Learning Strategy: Individual project, discussion.

Resources:

Maps of library media center (see pages 48 and 49).

List of library media center areas (see page 50).

Signs or labels in the areas (use what your center provides).

Methods:

The teacher will:
1. Review mapping skills.
2. Schedule classes in the library media center.
3. Have students hold maps and locate NORTH.
4. Give assistance to students.

The library media specialist will:
1. Make outline maps of the library media center.
2. Prepare a list of library media center areas.
3. Prepare signs or labels for any areas needing them.
4. Prepare transparencies showing location of areas.
5. Lead discussion about location of resources.   (Text continues on page 51.)

Map of Hammond Middle School Library Media Center

Map of Media Center with Auxiliary Rooms

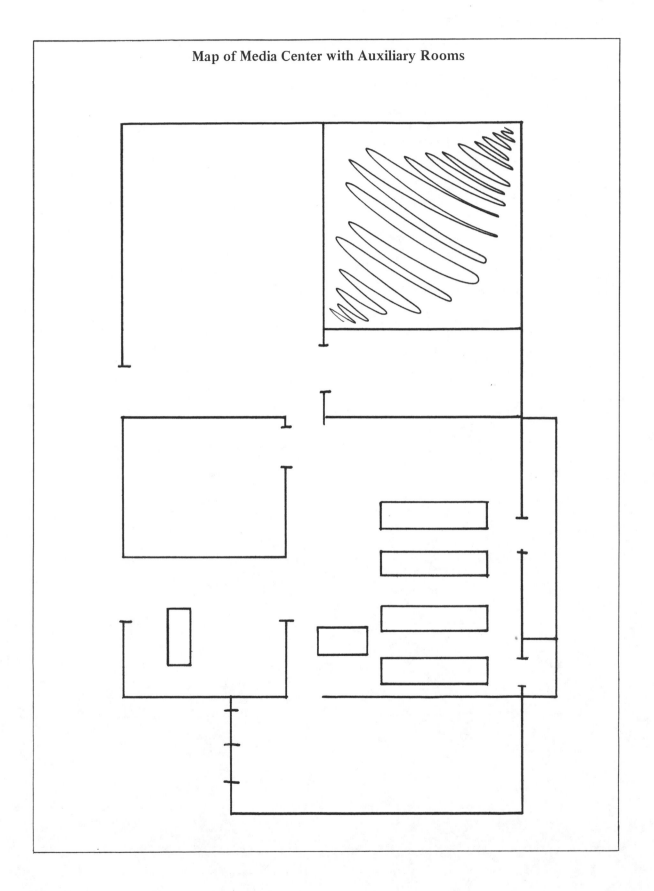

Hammond Middle School Library Media Center Areas

Magazines.

Fiction.

Reference.

Circulation Desk.

Card Catalog.

TV Area.

Class Area.

Vertical File.

Encyclopedias.

920 921 (Biography).

000 (General Works).

100 (Philosophy).

200 (Religion).

300 (Social Science).

400 (Language).

500 (Pure Science).

600 (Technology).

700 (The Arts).

800 (Literature).

900 (History).

Nonprint Material.

Equipment.

TV Studio.

Darkroom.

Methods (cont'd.)

The students will:

1. Complete the map of the library media center by labeling the areas where resources are located.

2. Discuss the location of the areas and the purposes of the areas with the library media specialist in a large group session.

3. Check and correct map using the transparency projected by the library media specialist.

4. File the completed map in the student handbook.

Evaluative Criteria: The students will correctly label the map of the library media center identifying the physical location of resources.

LESSON 4

Title: Equipment Operation: Easy as 1, 2, 3.

Overview: The purpose of this unit is to teach students the basic principles of operating audiovisual equipment. Students will follow directions for operating equipment at the learning centers.

Library Media Skills Objectives:

Operate: 16-mm projector, 8-mm cartridge projector, overhead projector, cassette recorder, filmstrip projector, microfiche projector, slide projector, video tape recorder, opaque projector.

Performance Objective: Given a demonstration lesson on video tape of the basic principles of operating audiovisual equipment and given learning centers containing diagrams and charts of operating procedures, the students will operate at least ten types of audiovisual equipment in the library media center.

Subject Area: Industrial Arts.

Learning Strategy: Demonstration, audiovisual instruction, practice.

Resources:

Manual of instruction from manufacturers.

Diagrams of equipment with parts labeled.

Charts of operating procedures.

Video tape of demonstration lesson.

Equipment and nonprint material for each piece of equipment.

Directions for Operating Audiovisual Equipment.

Methods:

The teacher will:
1.　Discuss the importance of learning the care and operation of audiovisual equipment.
2.　Stress the significance of *following directions* for all industrial arts activities.
3.　State that the basic principles of operating any equipment require careful attention to safety rules, familiarity with all parts, and a systematic or logical procedure of operation.
4.　Divide class into groups of three.
5.　Schedule classes in the library media center for several class periods until all students complete the ten learning centers.

The library media specialist will:
1.　Have diagrams of equipment and charts of operation made by student aides or industrial arts students using the equipment manuals from the manufacturers. They may use the opaque projector.
2.　Laminate the charts and diagrams.
3.　Set up ten learning centers with equipment and nonprint material.
4.　Ask student library media aide and the industrial arts teacher to assist at the learning centers and to verify the students' operation procedures.
5.　Give an operator's license to each student who successfully completes the ten learning centers.

Directions for Operating Audiovisual Equipment

1. Look at the diagram of the equipment. Read the labels on each part.

2. Look at the piece of equipment. Identify each part.

3. Read the operating instructions *carefully*.

4. Follow directions: as 1, 2, 3.

5. Never force anything.

6. Ask for assistance with *any* problem.

**Sample
Operator's License**

_____Bill Smith_____

has successfully completed

the Audiovisual Course

at

Hammond Middle School.

_____L Van Vliet_____
Library Media Specialist

_____10/23/83_____

Methods (cont'd.)

The students will:

1. View the video tape demonstration.
2. Work with group to complete assignment at each station.
3. Receive Operator's Licenses.
4. Assist with operation of equipment in class.
5. Operate equipment in learning centers.

Evaluative Criteria: The students will correctly operate the audiovisual equipment at all ten learning centers.

Special Note: Students who have reading problems will need extra assistance with the stations. The operating procedures could be taped for them.

LESSON 5

Title: It's a Matter of Fact.

Overview: The primary purpose of this unit is to assist students in locating and utilizing nonfiction materials. The secondary purpose is to familiarize students with the variety of informative and fascinating nonfiction materials.

Library Media Skills Objectives:

Distinguish between fiction and nonfiction.

Locate nonfiction collection: print and nonprint.

Use card catalog to find available material on a subject.

Use cross references: *See* and *See also.*

Use call numbers to locate nonfiction material.

Gain information from nonfiction materials.

Choose reading as a leisure-time activity.

Choose listening and viewing of nonprint materials as a leisure-time activity.

Performance Objective: Given information on nonfiction materials in the filmstrips *The World of Media* and *Media Organization* and given three task cards, the students will use the card catalog to locate at least one print or nonprint resource for each task card. They will complete an "It's a Matter of Fact" card for each resource.

Subject Area: Language Arts.

Learning Strategy: Audiovisual instruction, discussion, practice.

Resources:

Filmstrips: *The World of Media.* Encyclopaedia Britannica Educational Corp., 1974.

Media Organization: Nonfiction. Encyclopaedia Britannica Educational Corp., 1974.

Card catalog.

Nonfiction book collection.

Nonprint collection.

Task cards (see page 56).

"It's a Matter of Fact" cards (see page 57).

(Text continues on page 58.)

Task Cards

Race Cars	Trolley Cars	Sign Language	Major League Baseball
Motorcycles	San Francisco	Braille	Baseball Cards
Motorcross	Railroads	The Devil's Triangle	Circus
Engines	Helicopters	Pets	Pony Express
Solar Energy	Houdini	Ghosts	Inventions
Religion	Coin Collecting	Morse Code	Metric System
Guns	Jokes	Kites	Flying Saucers
Weapons	Tall Tales	Costumes	Russia
Annapolis	Myths	Civil War	Knights
Norsemen	Fairy Tales	World War II	Castles
Tractors	Riddles	Airplanes	Cartoons
Textiles	Astrology	Submarine	Babe Ruth
Golf	Movies	Sculpture	Billie Jean King
Nuclear Weapons	Hunting	Stamp Collecting	National Parks
Toboggan	Fishing	Turkeys	Limericks
Women's Suffrage	Soccer	Snacks	Williamsburg
Human Body	Computers	Birds	Egypt
Diets	Famous Gunfighters	Shells	Plays
Money	Photography	Trees	Pyramid
Poland	Artists	Pandas	Diseases
Fingerprinting	Pirates	Calligraphy	Trademarks
Trucks	Sunken Treasure	Martin Luther King	Indian Foods
Chemistry	Presidents	Middle Ages	Cookbooks
The Moon	The White House	Renaissance	Japan
Constellations	Supreme Court Decisions		

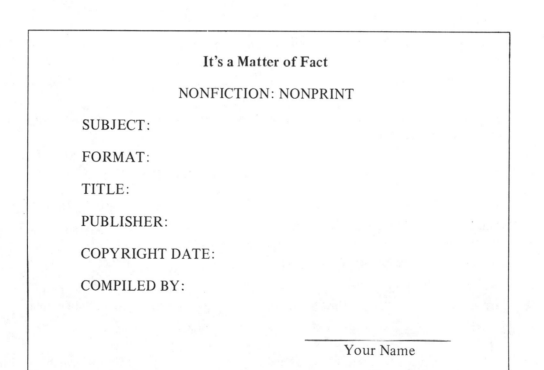

It's a Matter of Fact

NONFICTION: PRINT

SUBJECT:

CALL NUMBER:

TITLE:

AUTHOR:

PUBLISHER:

COPYRIGHT DATE:

COMPILED BY:

_____
Your name

It's a Matter of Fact

NONFICTION: NONPRINT

SUBJECT:

FORMAT:

TITLE:

PUBLISHER:

COPYRIGHT DATE:

COMPILED BY:

_____
Your Name

Methods:

The teacher will:

1. Plan the unit with the library media specialist as a part of sixth grade orientation to the library media center.
2. Schedule three class periods in the library media center.
3. Accompany class to the media center.
4. Evaluate lesson with library media specialist.

The library media specialist will:

1. Show and discuss the filmstrip *World of Media.*
2. Show and discuss the filmstrip *Media Organization: Nonfiction.*
3. Prepare approximately one hundred task cards listing topics for students to locate in the card catalog.
4. Prepare approximately one hundred "It's a Matter of Fact" cards.
5. Let students draw three task cards from a large box decorated with words like: information, data, nonfiction, facts.
6. Explain that students are to use the card catalog including the *see* and *see also* references to locate at least one resource for their topic.
7. Show the students the "It's a Matter of Fact" cards and demonstrate how a card is to be completed.
8. Remind the students that they should use the call number to locate the resource if it is on the shelf.
9. Allow students to browse through resources after they complete the "It's a Matter of Fact" cards.
10. Collect the completed cards and alphabetize cards by subject. Place in a box labeled "It's a Matter of Fact."
11. Tell students that they may use the cards to locate many fascinating nonfiction materials to use for their leisure time.

The students will:

1. Choose three task cards.
2. Use the card catalog to find at least one resource for each task card.
3. Make an "It's a Matter of Fact" card for each resource using the correct card for print or nonprint resources.
4. Locate and browse through resource.
5. Check out resource, if desired.
6. Turn in completed "It's a Matter of Fact" cards to the library media specialist.
7. Use file of "It's a Matter of Fact" cards to locate material for leisure use.

Evaluative Criteria: The students will use the card catalog to locate print and nonprint resources and complete "It's a Matter of Fact" cards.

LESSON 6

Title: Classification Systems—Scientific Know-How.

Overview: The purpose of this lesson is to help students learn the basis for classification by observing order, relationship, and patterns in objects found in the outdoor environment. The students will collect objects such as rocks, leaves, or seeds and devise a classification system to arrange the objects into related groups. This lesson could be taught by the library media specialist at an outdoor education program or on a field trip.

Library Media Skills Objectives:

Identify classification systems.

Select material based on specific criteria.

Arrange materials using a specific system.

Performance Objective: Given background information on classification systems, a set of guidelines, and materials to hold collected objects, the students will work with a partner to collect objects such as rocks, leaves, or seeds and devise a classification system to arrange objects.

Subject Area: Science.

Learning Strategy: Discussion, field trip, demonstration.

Resources:

Several sample collections of nuts, rocks, or leaves.

Bags or boxes for collections.

Cards and pencils.

Guidelines for collections and classifying (see page 60).

Methods:

The teacher will:

1. Review discussion notes, guidelines, and objectives that were written by the library media specialist.
2. Make suggestions and/or comments.
3. Review and evaluate lesson after it is taught.

The library media specialist will:

1. Lead students in a discussion of the needs for classification:
    Establish order.
    Find patterns and relationships.
2. Define classification.
    Classification is an act or method of arranging objects in groups:
    *   Objects can be grouped by common properties.
    *   Objects can be grouped in categories that are meaningful, useful, and consistent.
    *   No one way of grouping is correct.
    Show examples of nuts or leaves and let students tell how they could be classified.

Guidelines for Collections and Classifying

Guidelines for Collections:

1. Choose an object such as a rock and try to find at least five different types of rocks.

2. Study the objects to see how they are related.

3. Collect objects that are small enough to carry easily.

4. Be careful not to choose poisonous objects.

5. You may want to make brief notes on cards about your collection.

6. Always stay within sight of your teacher.

Guidelines for Classifying:

1. Study the properties of the objects you have collected.

2. Place objects in groups that have one or more characteristics in common: size, color, shape, texture, use, type.

3. Write your classification system on a card.

4. Tell how you grouped your objects.

5. Show your objects and share your classification system with the entire group.

Methods (cont'd.)

3. Briefly discuss and review the Dewey Decimal Classification System stressing the contribution by Melvil Dewey.

4. Ask students to explain how materials are organized in a music store. Give suggestions to add to student comments. Materials can be arranged by:
   Format: cassettes (mono, stereo); records (speed—45, 33, singles, albums); sheet music (piano, guitar).
   Type of music: Classical, Jazz, Bluegrass, Rock (sub-grouped by composer, performer).

5. Discuss the many ways that weather can be classified:
   Seasons: properties of spring, summer, autumn, winter.
   Storms: cyclones, tornadoes, hurricanes, floods.
   Symbols: cloud cover, rain, snow.
   Fronts: warm, cold, stationary, occluded.
   Cloud Forms: cirrus, stratus, cumulus, and others.

6. Divide students into groups of two.

7. Give students guidelines for collecting objects and for classifying them.

8. Accompany students to an area for collection of objects.

9. Distribute materials to hold collections.

10. After students have collected objects, take them to an area where they can devise their classification system.

11. Have each group show their collection and tell how they classified it.

12. Each group should be successful since there is no right way for grouping.

13. If there is time, ask students other ways that collections could be grouped or classified.

The students will:

1. Discuss and define classification systems.

2. Read guidelines for collection and classification.

3. Work with a partner to collect related objects for classification. (Suggestions for objects to collect: soil, rocks, wildflowers, weeds, leaves, grass, pods, roots, seeds, bark, cones.)

4. Devise a classification system.

5. Show a collection and explain classification system.

Time Table: Approximately 1 hour 30 minutes.

(30 minutes)   1.   Discussion, demonstration, guidelines.

(30 minutes)   2.   Collecting.

(15 minutes)   3.   Classifying.

(15 minutes)   4.   Group time, sharing.

Evaluative Criteria: The students will work with a partner to collect a group of objects and will successfully classify these objects.

LESSON 7

Title: Biography: Footprints.

Overview: The purpose of this lesson is to have students locate, select, and read a biography about someone they would like to have known. They will present an oral character sketch of this person based on the point of view of the author.

Library Media Skills Objectives:

Locate materials using call numbers.

Select many different types of books according to reading level and interest.

Identify and describe the point of view.

Performance Objective: Given an introductory lesson on interesting people and the call number of biographies, the students will locate, select, and read a biography and present an oral report.

Subject Area: Reading.

Learning Strategy: Book talk, reading, practice.

Resources:

Biography Worksheet. (See page 63.)

Biography Collection: Collective biographies and individual biographies.

Index to Collective Biography for Young Readers.

Methods:

The teacher will:
1.   Review plans of the library media specialist for the introductory lesson.
2.   Schedule two class periods in the library media center.
3.   Select and read a biography and give an oral presentation along with the students.
4.   Evaluate student presentations.

The library media specialist will:
1.   Present an introductory lesson:
   •   Give the students the Biography Worksheet of interesting people and have them match biographical data with names. Tell them to guess if they do not know the answers.
   •   Have biographies already arranged on a display rack in numerical order of the entries on the biography worksheet. Bring out the rack after the students have completed the worksheet.
   •   Show each book and ask students to supply the biographical data. Fill in additional data. Give several examples of the author's point of view.
   •   Discuss the call numbers for collective and individual biographies. Ask students to give the call number for five of the books on display.

Biography Worksheet

Match the following names with the biographical data.

_____ 1. Louisa May Alcott	a. First woman doctor
_____ 2. P. T. Barnum	b. Inventor of the famous bowie knife
_____ 3. Evangeline Booth	c. Author of *Little Women*
_____ 4. Nathaniel Bowditch	d. A great showman, producer of the "Greatest Show on Earth"
_____ 5. Elizabeth Blackwell	e. An industrial engineer in the scientific management field whose story is told in *Cheaper by the Dozen*
_____ 6. Aaron Burr	
_____ 7. Frank Gilbreth, Jr.	f. Woman preacher and crusader for social and economic reform
_____ 8. Winston Churchill	g. Author of the *American Practical Navigator* known as the Sailor's Bible
_____ 9. Gandhi	h. Developed a system of dots for use in books for the blind
_____ 10. James Bowie	
_____ 11. Thomas Dooley, M.D.	i. Traitor, vice president, who killed his rival in a duel
_____ 12. Walt Frazier	j. A scientist and writer who shocked Americans into reevaluating the man-made chemicals that have polluted our environment
_____ 13. Madame Curie	
_____ 14. Louis Braille	
_____ 15. Confucius	k. Carthaginian general
_____ 16. Martin Luther	l. Wife of a U. S. President, crusader
_____ 17. Albert Schweitzer	m. Leader of the Reformation
_____ 18. Maria Tallchief	n. A young boy who died
_____ 19. Cleopatra	o. Prime minister of Great Britain 1940-45 and 1951-55
_____ 20. Hannibal	
_____ 21. Eleanor Roosevelt	p. Great doctor in Africa, humanitarian, philosopher
_____ 22. Laura Ingalls Wilder	q. Great teacher in China
_____ 23. Johnny Gunther	r. A great scientist, discoverer of radium
_____ 24. Rachel Carson	s. Navy doctor among Vietnamese
	t. Queen of Egypt
	u. A prima ballerina
	v. Author of *Little House on the Prairie*
	w. Great soul, "Saint of India"
	x. Great guard of the N. B. A.

Answer key on page 64.

Methods (cont'd.)

2. Give individual reading assistance to students to help them select an interesting biography.
3. Evaluate oral presentations.

The students will:

1. Complete the biography worksheet.
2. Discuss answers with the library media specialist.
3. Locate and select a biography.
4. Read a biography.
5. Plan a character sketch based on the biography.
   Include name, birth date, occupation, nationality, major accomplishments, obstacles over-come, several interesting facts or happenings, title of biography, author.
   (Students may dress in costumes and include pictures or illustrations.)

Evaluative Criteria: The students will complete the biography worksheet; locate, select, and read a biography, and present an oral character sketch based on the author's point of view.

Answer key for Biography Worksheet (see page 63): 1c, 2d, 3f, 4g, 5a, 6i, 7e, 8o, 9w, 10b, 11s, 12x, 13r, 14h, 15q, 16m, 17p, 18u, 19t, 20k, 21l, 22v, 23n, 24j.

LESSON 8

Title: Astronomy: Out of This World.

Overview: The purpose of this lesson is to guide students in the location and use of print and non-print materials on astronomy for a science project.

Library Media Skills Objectives:

Use Dewey Decimal System of Classification to locate materials.

Interpret information found in resources.

Performance Objective: Given information on the Dewey Decimal System of Classification and an overview of information on astronomy, the students will locate and use print and nonprint materials on astronomy to produce a project.

Subject Area: Science.

Learning Strategy: Lecture, practice, project.

Resources:

Dewey Decimal System of Classification.

Books: Gallant, Roy. *The Constellations: How They Came to Be.*

Iver, David. *Dictionary of Astronomy: Space and Atmospheric Phenomena.*

Jobb, Jamie. *The Night Sky Book.*

Limburg, Peter. *What's in the Name of Stars and Constellations?*

Branley, Franklyn. *Jupiter.*

Asimov, Issac. *Venus, Near Neighbor of the Sun.*

Couper, Heater, and Terrence Murtagh. *Heavens Above.*

Richardson, Robert. *The Stars and Serendipity.*

Berger, Melvin. *Quasars, Pulsars and Black Holes.*

National Geographic. *Picture Atlas of Our Universe.*

Filmstrips: *Astronomy.* National Geographic Learning Shelf.

The Universe. National Geographic.

Film Loops: *Solar System.* Encyclopaedia Britannica.

Planetary Motions. Encyclopaedia Britannica.

Pamphlets: NASA Educational Publications.

Encyclopedias.

Methods:

The teacher will:

1. Introduce the lesson.
2. Give examples of student projects.

Possible Projects

Model of planets

Chart of characteristics of planets

An astrolabe

A report showing difference between stars and planets or a galaxy and a constellation

Computer graphics

Animated movie

Slide/tape

The library media specialist will:

1. Present information on the Dewey Decimal System of Classification:

    500 Science.
    503 Dictionaries, Encyclopedias.
    508 Collections, Anthologies.
    520 Astronomy.
    521 Theoretical Astronomy and Celestial Mechanics.
    522 Practical and Spherical Astronomy.
    523 Descriptive Astronomy.

2. Give a brief overview of information on astronomy from print and nonprint sources.

3. Assist with research and projects.

The students will:

1. Locate print and nonprint materials on astronomy.

2. Interpret information found in resources.

3. Plan, organize, and present a project.

Evaluative Criteria: The students will locate and utilize information on astronomy to produce a project.

LESSON 9

Title: Tumbling On!

Overview: The purpose of this lesson is to help students increase motor skills for gymnastic routines by viewing a video tape of themselves performing selected routines.

Library Media Skills Objectives:

Use appropriate A-V equipment for selected presentation.

Operate a video recorder.

Performance Objective: Given a video tape of their class performing gymnastic routines, the students will operate the video recorder and will locate, view, and critique their routine.

Subject Area: Physical Education.

Learning Strategy: Practice, audiovisual instruction.

Methods:

The teacher will:
1. Teach gymnastic routines to students.
2. Schedule video taping sessions with the library media specialist.
3. Schedule individual video tape playback sessions with the library media specialist.

The library media specialist will:
1. Arrange for student library media technicians to videotape gymnastic practice sessions.
2. Keep a log of names of individuals who are being videotaped.
3. Schedule individuals for playback of video tapes.
4. Instruct each student in techniques for operating the video recorder for playbacks.

The students will:
1. Practice a gymnastic routine and perform for a video tape session.
2. Check the log for name and location of individual routine on video tape.
3. Receive instruction in operating the video recorder for a playback.
4. View and critique their own video taped routines.
5. Practice routine to make improvements after viewing video tape.

Evaluative Criteria: The students will correctly operate the video recorder to locate, view, and critique their gymnastic routines.

LESSON 10

Title: ABC's of Alphabetizing.

Overview: The purpose of this lesson is to review alphabetizing skills to help students locate information in the resources of the library media center.

Library Media Skills Objectives:

Alphabetize list of authors by last name.

Alphabetize titles.

Distinguish between word-by-word and letter-by-letter alphabetizing.

Performance Objective: Given a list of authors' names and a list of titles of books, the students will arrange each list in alphabetical order. Given a sample of word-by-word and letter-by-letter alphabetizing, the students will distinguish between them.

Subject Area: Language Arts.

Learning Strategy: Demonstration, game, practice.

Resources:

Worksheet 1, list of authors' names. (See page 69.)

Worksheet 2, list of titles of books. (See page 69.)

Worksheet 3, list of topics arranged word-by-word and letter-by-letter. (See page 69.)

Three sets of letters of the alphabet on cards approximately 8" x 10" (one large letter on each card).

Transparencies: Authors' names. (See page 69.)

Example of word-by-word and letter-by-letter alphabetizing. (See page 69.)

Methods:

The teacher will:

1.   Plan the lesson with the library media specialist.
2.   Schedule the classes in the library media center.
3.   Plan follow-up activities in the classroom.

Worksheet 1

Arrange the authors' names in alphabetical order.

London, Jack	L'Engle, Madeline
Byars, Betsy	White, T. H.
White, E. B.	Wyss, Johann
Paterson, Katherine	Le Guin, Ursula
Hamilton, Virginia	Hamilton, Edith
Konigsburg, E. L.	Patterson, Lillie

Worksheet 2

Arrange the titles in alphabetical order.

Zeely	*Julie of the Wolves*
Summer of the Swans	*Old Yeller*
Where the Lilies Bloom	*A Long Way to Whiskey Creek*
The Little Prince	*Deenie*
The Phantom Tollbooth	*The Great Gilly Hopkins*
The Greenwitch	*Child of the Owl*
The Gray King	*M. C. Higgins, the Great*
The Tombs of Atuan	

Worksheet 3

Identify the alphabetical arrangement as *A*—word-by-word or *B*—letter-by-letter.

American	American
Americana	American Art
American Art	American Legion
American Legion	Americana
Fort Dodge	Fort Dodge
Forte	Fort Knox
Forth	Fort Wayne
Fort Knox	Forte
Fort Wayne	Forth

Methods (cont'd.)

The library media specialist will:

1. Make lists of authors' names, titles of books, and examples of word-by-word and letter-by-letter alphabetizing for worksheets 1, 2, and 3.

2. Prepare three sets of alphabet cards.

3. Introduce the lesson with a review of alphabetizing skills:
   - Make a transparency and cut it into strips.
   - Arrange strips in alphabetical order.
   - Show a transparency of an example of word-by-word and letter-by-letter alphabetizing.

4. Play a game: Alphabetical Order.
   - Divide students into two teams.
   - Give each member a card with a large letter of the alphabet.
   - Give cards in random order.
   - Arrange teams in two rows.
   - Hold up a card with a letter.
   - Ask students from each team to stand if they have the letter that comes *before* that letter.
   - Give a point to the first team to get the correct answers.
   - Go through the alphabet twice.
   - Give five points to the team that correctly arrange themselves in alphabetical order.

5. Ask students to complete the worksheets.

6. Grade the worksheets.

7. Discuss the evaluations of the worksheet with the teacher for follow-up activities by the teacher.

The students will:

1. Observe the demonstration lesson.

2. Play the alphabetical order game.

3. Complete the worksheets.

Evaluative Criteria: The students will correctly complete the worksheets using the techniques of alphabetization.

LESSON 11

Title: African Nations: Fascinating Facts.

Overview: The purpose of this lesson is to help each student identify, locate, select, interpret, and utilize facts about a country in Africa by completing a booklet. Many library media skills can be incorporated into this social studies unit.

Library Media Skills Objectives:

Identify and locate the card catalog, the vertical file, periodicals, newspapers, encyclopedias, almanacs, atlases, special dictionaries, filmstrips, and tapes.

Select an encyclopedia, an almanac, a filmstrip, and a dictionary to find information on a given subject.

Interpret maps, graphs, and charts.

Compare facts from different sources.

Use an index.

Summarize information.

Prepare a bibliography.

Performance Objective: Given directions for completing a project booklet on a country in Africa, the student will utilize the resources in the library media center to correctly compile factual information.

Subject Area: Social Studies.

Learning Strategy: Lecture, demonstration, project.

Resources:

Encyclopedias, almanacs, dictionaries, atlases, filmstrips, tapes, vertical file, newspapers, magazines.

Transparency of map of Africa.

Record: *Around Africa in Song.* Columbia Master Works.

Project Guidelines (see page 72).

Sample Booklet (see page 73).

Bibliographic Form

(Text continues on page 74.)

Project Guidelines

Follow these directions for each page:

Page 1:   Name of country

Flag

Your name and section number

Page 2:   Facts-in-Brief:

Area in square miles

Capital city

Population

Official language

Page 3:   Geography

Climate

Topography

Page 4:   Resources

Page 5:   Famous people

Page 6:   Historical events

Page 7:   Housing

Page 8:   Transportation

Page 9:   Government

Page 10:   Schools

Page 11:   Current events

Page 12:   Bibliography

Sample Booklet: African Nations

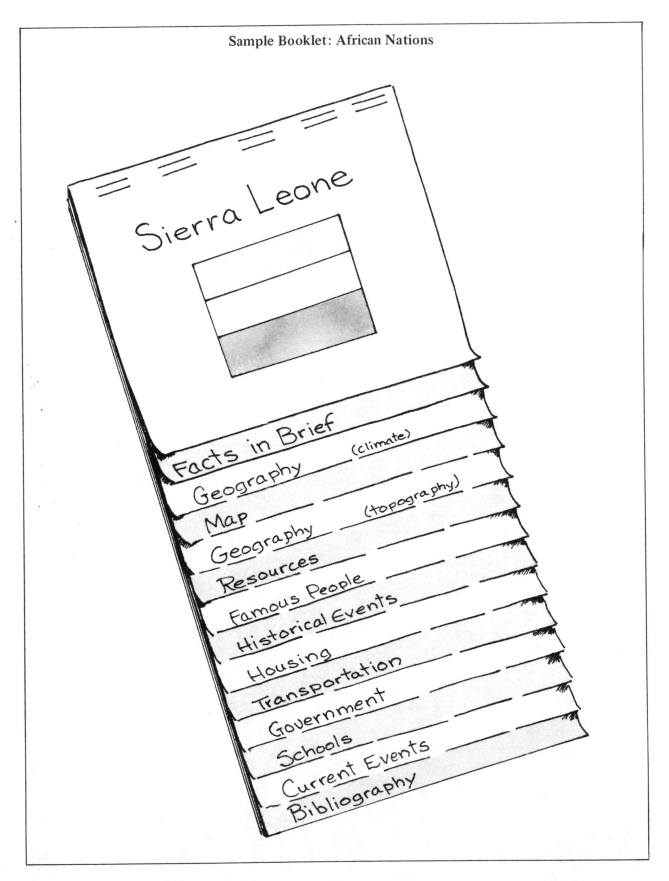

Methods:

The teacher will:

1. Assign topic (country of Africa); show transparency of map of Africa; and play record.
2. Distribute project guidelines.
3. Show sample booklet.
4. Schedule five class periods in the library media center.
5. Assist with research.
6. Provide materials for booklet.
7. Grade project.

The library media specialist will:

1. Review location of library media center resources.
2. Instruct students in the use of almanacs, special encyclopedias, and atlases.
3. Give individual reference assistance as needed.
4. Explain the bibliographic format.
5. Evaluate project.

The students will:

1. View transparency of map of Africa and listen to record *Around Africa in Song.*
2. Observe demonstration.
3. Locate and utilize information.
4. Complete project booklet.

Evaluative Criteria: The student will complete a project booklet using correct facts.

LESSON 12

Title: Books: Page after Page.

Overview: The purpose of this lesson is to extend the students' knowledge of the parts of books to enable them to more fully utilize all parts of books.

Library Media Skills Objective:

Identify and use all parts of a book.

Performance Objective: Given information on the parts of books in a learning center, the students will complete a worksheet utilizing all parts of a book.

Subject Area: Language Arts.

Learning Strategy: Learning center.

Resources:

Learning center with illustrations of parts of book (see pages 76 and 77).

Cover, spine, call number, body or text.

Title page.

Copyright page.

Dedication.

Preface, foreword, or introduction.

Table of contents.

List of illustrations or maps.

Body or text.

Appendix.

Glossary.

Bibliography.

Index.

Methods:

The teacher will:

1.   Introduce the objectives.
2.   Schedule students on a rotating basis to complete the learning center in the library media center.
3.   Use follow-up activities in future assignments utilizing the parts of books.

(Text continues on page 78.)

Illustration of Parts of a Book

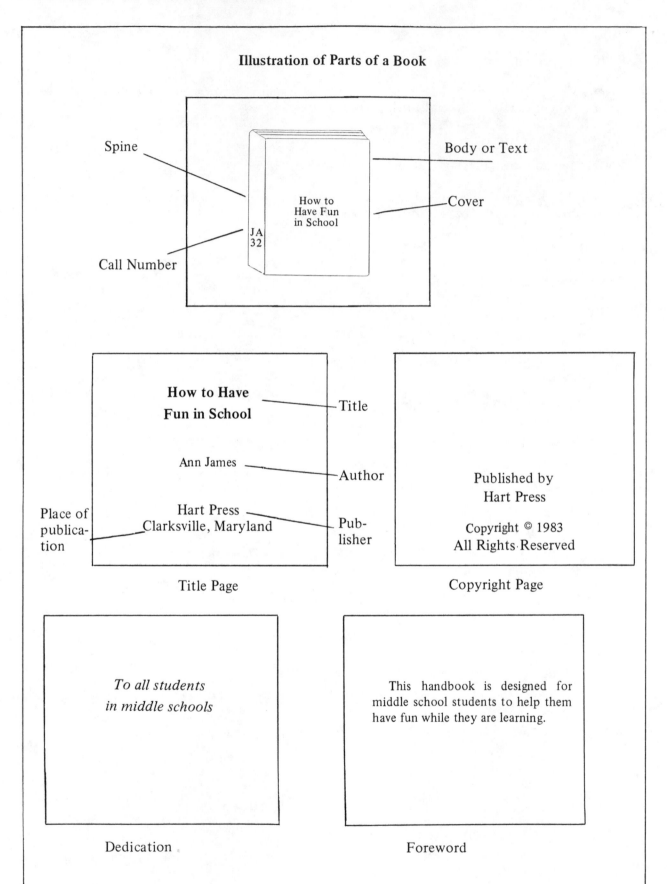

Spine

Body or Text

Cover

How to
Have Fun
in School

JA
32

Call Number

How to Have
Fun in School — Title

Ann James — Author

Place of
publica-
tion

Hart Press
Clarksville, Maryland — Publisher

Title Page

Published by
Hart Press

Copyright © 1983
All Rights Reserved

Copyright Page

*To all students
in middle schools*

Dedication

This handbook is designed for middle school students to help them have fun while they are learning.

Foreword

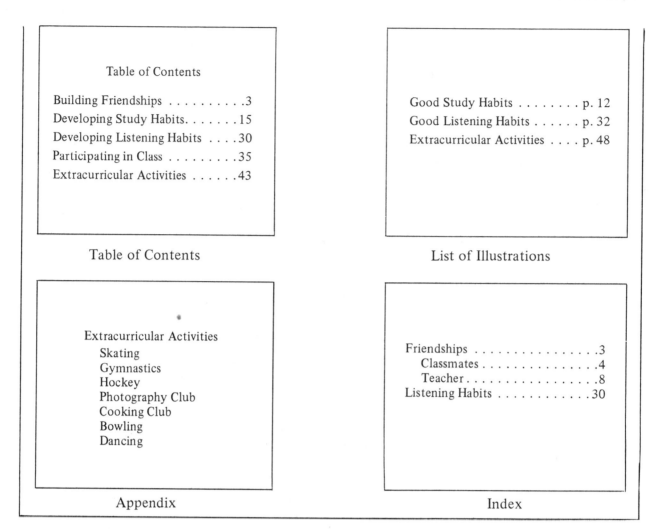

Table of Contents

Building Friendships 3
Developing Study Habits. 15
Developing Listening Habits 30
Participating in Class 35
Extracurricular Activities 43

Table of Contents

Good Study Habits . . . . p. 12
Good Listening Habits . . . . . . p. 32
Extracurricular Activities . . . . p. 48

List of Illustrations

Extracurricular Activities
   Skating
   Gymnastics
   Hockey
   Photography Club
   Cooking Club
   Bowling
   Dancing

Appendix

Friendships 3
   Classmates 4
   Teacher. 8
Listening Habits 30

Index

Work Sheet for Parts of a Book

Select a nonfiction book from the library media center. Use your own paper to answer the following questions about the book you have chosen:

1. What is the title?

2. Who is the author?

3. What is the call number?

4. Who is the publisher?

5. What is the copyright date?

6. Find the table of contents and list the first two entries.

7. List the page number where the main body or text begins.

8. List the following items if found in your book: preface, foreword, introduction, dedication, glossary, bibliography, index.

Methods (cont'd.)

The library media specialist will:

1. Make an attractive, colorful, learning center with illustrations of the parts of books.
2. Prepare the worksheet for students' use at the learning center.
3. Check and grade the worksheets.
4. Go over incorrect answers with students.
5. Evaluate the learning center with the teacher.

The students will:

1. Read the background information at the learning center.
2. Select a nonfiction book from the media center.
3. Complete the worksheet.
4. Refer any questions about parts of books to the library media specialist.

Evaluative Criteria: The students will correctly answer all questions on the worksheet utilizing all parts of a book.

LESSON 13

Title: Chilling, Thrilling Mysteries

Overview: The primary purpose of this lesson is to entertain students by telling them a scary story at Halloween. The secondary purpose is to promote listening skills and an appreciation for the art of storytelling.

Library Media Skills Objectives:

Identify an audio sequence of events.

Select reading as a personal activity.

Performance Objective: Given a Halloween setting and a scary story told by the library media specialist, the students will practice listening skills to identify an audio sequence of events.

Subject Area: Reading.

Learning Strategy: Oral presentation.

Resources:

Books: *Alfred Hitchcock's Witch's Brew.*
Alfred Hitchcock's Ghostly Gallery.
Alfred Hitchcock's Daring Detectives.
Alfred Hitchcock's Supernatural Tales of Terror and Suspense.
Alfred Hitchcock's Tales to Fill You with Fear and Trembling.

Cassette: Sound effects of scary music or of a haunted house.

Black costume.

Jack-o'-lantern.

Small flashlight.

Methods:

The teacher will:
1. Review listening skills by stressing the importance of identifying a sequence of events.
2. Ask the students to listen carefully to the story that will be told to them by the library media specialist.
3. Schedule the class in the library media center.
4. Accompany the class and listen to the story.
5. Return to the classroom after the story and briefly discuss the sequence of events.

Methods (cont'd.)

The library media specialist will:

1. Select a story from one of Alfred Hitchcock's mystery series such as Burrage's *The Waxworks.*

2. Learn the story for a storytelling presentation.

3. Arrange chairs in a circle in a dark room.

4. Dress in a black costume.

5. Have a large jack-o'-lantern with a flashlight inside in the middle of the circle.

6. Greet students at the door of the darkened room and guide them to their seats.

7. Use a sound effects record of scary music or of a haunted house as background while students are being seated.

8. Introduce the story by telling the students some background information about Alfred Hitchcock and his scary movies. Tell them that he often uses a surprise ending in his movies. State that he did not write the stories in his mystery series but that he edited or selected stories written by many authors.

9. Give the author and title and tell the story.

10. Have a display of Alfred Hitchcock's books as well as other mystery stories in the library media center.

The student will:

1. Discuss listening skills.

2. Go to the library media center to hear a scary Halloween story.

3. Participate in a discussion of the sequence of events of the story.

4. Select a mystery story to read as an optional activity.

Evaluative Criteria: The students will listen to a scary story told by the library media specialist and will correctly identify the sequence of events.

LESSON 14

Title: Let's Visit Asia!

Overview: The purpose of this unit is to have students locate and utilize information on a selected Asian country. They will select a country, compile information, and prepare a news program for video taping.

Library Media Skills Objectives:

Locate and use almanacs, atlases, encyclopedias, periodicals, maps, filmstrips.

Performace Objective: Given a list of facts for research on an Asian country, the students will locate and utilize information from many sources. They will prepare a news program for video taping.

Subject Area: Social Studies.

Learning Strategy: Discussion, practice, project.

Resources:

Books: *The World Almanac.*
National Geographic Picture Atlas of Our World.
Rand McNally Cosmospolitan World Atlas.
Alexbank, Albert. *The China Challenge.*
Nance, John. *Land and People of the Philippines.*
World Book Encyclopedia.
Compton's Encyclopedia.

Chart: *China's People.* Encyclopaedia Britannica Educational Corp.

Record: *Japan—Its Sounds and People.* Capitol Records.

Magazines: *Newsweek, U. S. News and World Report, Time.*

List of Asian countries.

List of facts for research.

Methods:

The teacher will:

1.   Prepare a selected list of Asian countries for research.

Sample	
Japan	Indonesia
China	Malaysia
Korea	Taiwan
Philippines	

Methods (cont'd.)

2.   Prepare a list of issues for research.

Sample

Location	Religion
Capital	Housing
Climate	Education
Government	Current events
Language	Products
Topography	Natural Resources
Flag	

3.   Divide students into groups of five.

4.   Let each group choose a country for research.

5.   Schedule classes in library media center for research.

6.   Schedule classes for video taping.

7.   Evaluate video tapes with library media specialist.

The library media specialist will:

1.   Review the location and use of special reference books.

2.   Assist students in compiling data.

3.   Rehearse news program with students.

4.   Assign library media aides to video tape news programs.

The students will:

1.   Select an Asian country for research.

2.   Locate and utilize reference sources.

3.   Compile data.

4.   Prepare a storyboard for video news program.

5.   Prepare scenery, graphics, script.

6.   Rehearse scenes.

7.   Present news program for video taping.
- Make a title sign using name of country.
- Use national music for background.
- Dress in native or festival clothing.
- Have a large map and flag in background.
- Let weatherman describe climate, topography, and natural resources.
- Use an anchorman and several reporters to present information on the history, religion, education, housing, government, and current events.
- Use phrases or sayings in the various languages of the country.

Evaluative Criteria: The students will successfully locate and utilize information on an Asian country and will produce a video taped news program.

LESSON 15

Title: Kaleidoscope of Inventions.

Overview: The purpose of this lesson is to allow students to utilize locating and bibiographic skills to produce a card file on various inventions for later use for industrial arts projects.

Library Media Skills Objectives:

Locate a specific item of information in an index.

Locate illustrations.

Use vertical file to obtain materials.

Prepare a bibliography.

Performance Objective: Given a list of inventions, the students will locate information about them and will make a card file giving bibliographic information.

Subject Area: Industrial Arts.

Learning Strategy: Demonstration, practice.

Resources:

Books: Hayden, Robert. *Eight Black American Inventors.*
        Murphy, Jim. *Wierd and Wacky Inventions.*
        National Geographic. *More Inventive Americans.*
        Neal, Harry. *From Spinning Wheel to Spacecraft.*

Encyclopedias. '

List of inventions (see page 84).

Vertical file materials.

Bibliographic cards using 4" x 6" index cards (see page 84).

Transparency of a bibliographic card (see page 85).

Methods:

The teacher will:

1. Explain the purpose of the activity.
2. Give a list of inventions to each student.
3. Schedule classes to use the library media center.
4. Collect and file the completed cards.
5. At a later date let students use the cards to locate information for an industrial arts project.

List of Inventions

Sewing machine
Telephone
Telegraph
Phonograph
Laser
Amplifier
Television
Radio
Microphone
Reaper
Cotton Gin
Airplane
Automobile
Camera
Steam Engine
Elevator

(You can add many more inventions to the list according to the interests of your students.)

Sample Bibliography Card

SUBJECT: _____

AUTHOR: _____

TITLE: _____

PUBLISHER: _____

COPYRIGHT: _____

PAGES: _____

ILLUSTRATIONS: _____

Methods (cont'd.)

The library media specialist will:

1. Reserve books on inventions.
2. Review use of an index in books and encyclopedias.
3. Make bibliographic cards for students' use.
4. Demonstrate how to locate bibliographic information and transfer it to cards.
    - Show the book *Eight Black American Inventors* by Robert Hayden.
    - Look in the index to find the page numbers for the invention of the *first automated three-way traffic light.*
    - Turn to the title page of the book and locate the title, author, publisher. On the verso, locate the copyright date.
    - Complete the card on a transparency.

Sample Bibliography Card

SUBJECT: Traffic light

AUTHOR: Hayden, Robert

TITLE: Eight Black American Inventors

PUBLISHER: Addison-Wesley

COPYRIGHT: 1972

PAGES: 25-29

ILLUSTRATIONS: pp. 26-27

---

5. Assist students in locating and compiling bibliographic information.

The students will:

1. Select at least three inventions for research.
2. Locate information.
3. Compile information on cards.

Evaluative Criteria: The students will successfully locate information about inventions and will compile bibliographic data on cards.

LESSON 16

Title: Doing Your Thing.

Overview: The purpose of this unit is to motivate students to read independently by setting personal goals, selecting appropriate reading materials, and taking responsibility for meeting long-term deadlines.

Library Media Skills Objectives:

Select reading as a personal activity.

Select appropriate reading material.

Performance Objective: Given a book contract and guidelines for writing summaries, the students will set personal reading goals, sign a contract, select books from the library media center, and write a brief summary of each book read.

Subject Area: Reading.

Learning Strategy: Discussion, practice.

Resources:

Fiction and nonfiction book collection in the library media center.

Bibliographies.

Posters, displays.

Card catalog.

Book contract.

Guidelines for writing summaries.

Methods:

The teacher will:
1. Plan unit with the library media specialist.
2. Discuss objectives, activities, procedures, contracts, and guidelines for writing summaries with students.
3. Provide students with the opportunity to go to the media center to select books.
4. Grade summaries written by students.
5. Evaluate unit with library media specialist.

Book Contract

I agree to read _____ books for the stated period of January 1 to February 15, 1984. I will write a summary for each book read. I will receive a grade of A if I fulfill the contract.

_____
Student's Signature

Guidelines for Writing Summaries

Include the following:

1. Title of the book.

2. Name of the author.

3. List of the main characters.

4. Brief description of the main events.

5. Your opinion.

Methods (cont'd.)

The library media specialist will:

1. Discuss procedures for independent use of the library media center by students.
2. Prepare bibliographies for student use.
3. Promote reading by using attractive posters, displays, and learning centers.
4. Build a well-balanced collection of appropriate fiction and nonfiction books.
5. Read as many books as possible from the collections.
6. Give individual reading guidance if requested by students.
7. Review with the teacher summaries and opinions written by students.
8. Compile data about reading preferences of students.
9. Evaluate unit with teacher.

The students will:

1. Set individual goals for reading for a given time period.
2. Discuss the contract with the teacher and sign it after a three-day period for decision-making.
3. Select books from the library media center.
4. Keep a record of each book read.
5. Write a brief summary.
6. Rate each book numerically and state opinion of each book.
7. Turn in contract on specific due date.

Evaluative Criteria: The student will successfully complete the book contract.

LESSON 17

Title: It Pays to Listen.

Overview: The purpose of this lesson is to instruct students in the art of listening. To help them better understand the communication process, the students will diagram a communications model and explain the meaning of the terms. After a listening exercise, the students will identify the sequence of events.

Library Media Skills Objectives:

Identify an audio sequence of events.

Interpret a communications model.

Performance Objective: Given a communications model, the students will label the parts and explain the meaning of each part. They will listen to a recording and identify the sequence of events.

Subject Area: Language Arts.

Learning Strategy: Lecture, audiovisual instruction.

Resources:

Diagram of communications model.

Recordings: *Little House on the Prairie.* Newbery Award Records.
Short Stories of O. Henry. Listening Library.
Are You Listening? J. C. Penney Co.

Books: Mortensen, C. David. *Communication.*

Slide Tape: *Now Hear This! Becoming a Better Listener.* Center for Humanities.

Methods:

The teacher will:

1. Discuss the importance of listening skills with the students.
2. Ask the students to define *communication.*
3. Invite the library media specialist to come to the classroom to diagram and explain a simple communication model.
4. Have students listen to a recording and list a sequence of events.

The library media specialist will:

1. Diagram a simple communication model.

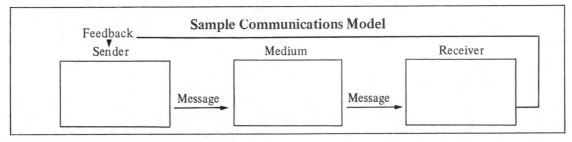

Methods (cont'd.)

2. Show the slide tape program *Now Hear This! Becoming a Better Listener.* At the end of each part interact with students by discussing ideas presented.

3. Give the teacher several recordings so that the teacher can pick one to use with the class.

4. Evaluate the lesson with the teacher.

The students will:

1. Label the parts of a communication model.

2. Explain the meaning of each part orally.

3. View a slide tape program. Discuss ideas.

4. Listen to a recording and make a list of the sequence of events.

Evaluative Criteria: The students will successfully label the parts of a communications model and orally explain their meanings. They will listen to a recording and list the sequence of events.

LESSON 18

Title: Step-by-Step.

Overview: The purpose of this lesson is to assist students with the planning and construction of a mural depicting symbols of their state.

Library Media Skills Objectives:

Select suitable source of information for a specified subject.

Infer facts and ideas from maps and charts.

Use appropriate A-V equipment for selected presentation.

Performance Objective: Given guidelines for constructing a mural, the students will design and construct a mural.

Subject Area: Art.

Learning Strategy: Practice, project.

Resources:

Books: Randall, Arne. *Murals for Schools.*
         National Geographic Picture Atlas of Our Fifty States.
         Brandt, Sue. *Facts about the 50 States.*
         Smith, Whitney. *Flag Book of the United States.*

Opaque projector.

Maps of states.

Methods:

The teacher will:
1.   Demonstrate the techniques and purposes of murals.
2.   Schedule reference sessions in the library media center.
3.   Critique mural designs of students that are drawn on large sheets of paper.
4.   Select best designs for actual mural paintings on wall of school.

The library media specialist will:
1.   Reserve books and nonprint materials.
2.   Assist students in locating symbols of their state.
3.   Demonstrate use of opaque projector.
4.   Evaluate lesson with the art teacher.

Methods (cont'd.)

The students will:

1.   View pictures and slides of murals.
2.   Practice drawing designs of murals.
3.   Locate pictures and descriptions of state symbols.
4.   Draw design of mural using large sheets of paper or use opaque projector to trace designs.
5.   Transfer design on wall by using opaque projector.

Evaluative Criteria: The students will plan and construct a mural depicting symbols of their state.

LESSON 19

Title: Going Places.

Overview: The purpose of this lesson is for students to use ideas and facts from fiction books on animals to compare and contrast with animals they observe on a field trip to the zoo.

Library Media Skills Objectives:

Compare ideas and facts for identity, difference, and contradiction.

Performance Objective: Given a fiction book on an animal and a field trip to the zoo, the students will read the book, will make a list of facts or ideas learned from the book, and will make comparisons and contrasts with their observations of the animal at the zoo.

Subject Area: Reading.

Learning Strategy: Reading, field trip.

Resources:

Books (examples):

Adams, Richard. *Watership Down.*

Annixter, J. *Sea Otter.*

Atwater, R. *Mr. Popper's Penguins.*

Baker, Betty. *Dupper.*

Burnford, S. *Incredible Journey.*

Christensen, G. *Buffalo Kill.*

Clarkson, E. *Halie: The Story of a Gray Seal.*

Dixon, P. *Silver Wolf.*

Dixon, P. *Summer of a White Goat.*

Ellis, M. *Caribou Crossing.*

Sad Song of the Coyote.

George, Jean. *Julie of the Wolves.*

Morey, Walt. *Canyon Winter.*

Pinkwater, D. Manus. *Lizard Music.*

Rawlings, Marjorie. *The Yearling.*

Cameras and film.

Maps of zoo.

Sketch pads.

Methods:

The teacher will:

1. Explain the purpose of the field trip to the zoo as a culminating activity for an interdisciplinary unit on animals where students have viewed movies and filmstrips, done research, and completed learning stations.

2. Ask students to select a fiction book on an animal from the library media center.

3. Give directions to students for making a list of facts and ideas obtained by reading the book on an animal.

4. Give students a map of the zoo and let them locate the area where the animal they are to observe will be.

5. Ask students to observe the habitat and characteristics of the animal at the zoo.

6. Have students complete a report comparing and contrasting the information from the fiction book with the observation of the animal at the zoo.

The library media specialist will:

1. Obtain a list of animals at the zoo.

2. Locate and reserve fiction books on the animals in the zoo: prairie dogs, rabbits, sea otters, penguins, seals, swans, goats, coyotes, deer.

3. Assist students with selection of fiction books.

4. Instruct students in use of cameras for picture taking at the zoo.

5. Plan to accompany the teacher and students on the field trip to the zoo.

6. Evaluate lesson with teacher.

The students will:

1. Select and read a fiction book from the reserved books on animals.

2. Make a list of characteristics based on the book.

3. Participate in the field trip to the zoo.

4. Observe the animal at the zoo.

5. Take photographs or sketch the animal.

6. Prepare an oral report comparing and contrasting the information obtained by reading about the animal to observing the animal at the zoo.

7. Show pictures or sketches of the animal.

Evaluative Criteria: The students will select and read a fiction book about an animal and will give an oral report comparing and contrasting the information from the book with an observation of the animal at the zoo.

LESSON 20

Title: Abridged or Unabridged?

Overview: The purpose of this lesson is to help students distinguish between the contents of abridged and unabridged resources in the library media center.

Library Media Skills Objectives:

Distinguish between content of abridged and unabridged resources.

Performance Objective: Given a demonstration lesson, the students will distinguish between abridged and unabridged resources.

Subject Area: Language Arts.

Learning Strategy: Demonstration, discussion.

Resources:

Webster's Third New International Dictionary.

Webster's Ninth New Collegiate Dictionary.

Readers' Guide to Periodical Literature.

Abridged Readers' Guide to Periodical Literature.

Reader's Digest Magazine.

Wyss, Johann. *The Swiss Family Robinson* (Abridged by Robert Larson).

Defoe, Daniel. *Robinson Crusoe* (Abridged by Audrey Butler).

Methods:

The teacher will:

1. Discuss the lesson with the library media specialist who will have the primary responsibility for teaching.
2. Schedule class in library media center.
3. Reinforce concepts during subsequent lessons.

The library media specialist will:

1. Gather examples of abridged and unabridged resources in the library media center. Do not display examples until the demonstration lesson.
2. Ask students to define *abridged* and *unabridged*.
   Let one student look up both words in an abridged dictionary.
   Let another student look up both words in an unabridged dictionary.
   Compare the answers.
3. Ask students to give examples of resources in the library media center that are abridged or unabridged.

Methods (cont'd)

4. Demonstrate abridged and unabridged resources by showing each resource and pointing out distinctive features, e.g.:

   Dictionaries—Give number of vocabulary entries.

   Readers' Guides—Give numbers of magazines indexed.

   Reader's Digest—Show one issue and give number of pages for an article, then show magazine article in original source and give number of pages.

   Novel: *Swiss Family Robinson*—Show abridged and unabridged editions.

5. Review lesson orally with students.

The student will:

1. Discuss abridged and unabridged resources in the library media center.

2. Distinguish between abridged and unabridged resources.

Evaluative Criteria: The students will distinguish between abridged and unabridged resources.

LESSON 21

Title: Getting to Know You.

Overview: The purpose of this lesson is for students to use a dictionary or thesaurus to find descriptive adjectives that express a positive quality or condition about the members of their sixth-grade class. This lesson should help the students, the teacher, and the library media specialist to learn more about each student.

Library Media Skills Objectives:

Use a dictionary.

Use a thesaurus.

Performance Objective: Given a list of the first names of all students in the class and a dictionary or thesaurus, the students will list at least one descriptive adjective—a positive quality—that expresses a condition about that student. The adjective must begin with the first letter of the student's name.

Subject Area: Language Arts.

Learning Strategy: Discussion, practice.

Resources:

Dictionaries.

Thesauruses.

List of students' first names.

Methods:

The teacher will:
1. Discuss the meaning of adjectives.
2. Ask for a definition of a descriptive adjective.
3. Ask what is meant by a *positive quality* as opposed to a *negative quality.*
4. Have students give examples of descriptive adjectives that express positive qualities, e.g., attractive, exciting, energetic.
5. Make a list of the first names of the students in the class.
6. Schedule the class to meet in the library media center.

The library media specialist will:
1. Reserve a dictionary and a thesaurus for each table.
2. Give out the list of students' names.
3. Collect the papers.
4. Play a game with the students by having them sit in a circle.

Methods (cont'd.)

5. Read a descriptive adjective and have the students say the name of the student to whom it could apply. The name must begin with the same letter as the adjective:

   enthralling—Edith or Eddy.
   happy—Helen or Henry.
   charming—Carol or Charles.
   delightful—Denise or David.
   lovely—Lucinda or Larry.
   alluring—Alice or Alan.

The students will:

1. Write a descriptive adjective beginning with the first letter of the students' first name.

2. Listen to the adjective and say the name of the student to whom it could apply.

Evaluative Criteria: The students will list a descriptive adjective that expresses a positive quality about each student.

LESSON 22

Title: Reading: A Lifetime Happening.

Overview: The purpose of this lesson is to challenge students to develop a positive attitude toward reading by utilizing a variety of reading materials needed to meet the demands of society.

Library Media Skills Objectives:

Select reading as a means of acquiring information.

Performance Objective: Given a worksheet after viewing a slide show, the students will list at least five answers for each category. They will compile a list of the varieties of the reading materials they use to meet their needs.

Subject Area: Reading.

Learning Strategy: Discussion, audiovisual presentation, practice.

Resources:

Slides of people reading.

Worksheet (see page 100).

Methods:

The teacher will:

1. Introduce the lesson by asking students to state several reasons for reading.
2. Discuss the questions the students will be asked to answer after viewing the slide presentation.
3. Collect and grade the worksheets.
4. Ask the students to do a homework assignment of compiling a list of the varieties of reading materials they use to meet their needs, e.g., *TV Guide*, menus, game instructions, labels, computer graphics, signs, charts.

The library media specialist will:

1. Collect slides of people reading.
2. Make title slides; select background music.
3. Present a slide program, *Reading: A Lifetime Happening*, showing people reading from youth to old age, in many places, for various reasons, and using a variety of media.

Methods (cont'd.)

The students will:

1. Complete the following worksheet after viewing the slide presentation.

Sample Worksheet		
Reading: A Lifetime Happening		
Places to read	Reasons for reading	Variety of reading materials

2. Compile a list of the varieties of reading materials they use to meet their needs.

Evaluative Criteria: The student will successfully complete the worksheet and the homework assignment.

LESSON 23

Title: You're Invited: Micro Demo.

Overview: The purpose of this unit is to provide students with the opportunity to develop computer literacy by identifying the parts of a microcomputer, learning about the care and handling of diskettes, and using the microcomputer to perform basic tasks.

Library Media Skills Objectives:

Identify a microcomputer.

Identify a diskette.

Operate a microcomputer.

Performance Objective: Given a video taped demonstration, the students will identify the parts of a microcomputer, will properly identify diskettes, and will use the microcomputer to perform basic tasks.

Subject Area: Mathematics.

Learning Strategy: Demonstration, practice.

Resources:

Video tape of demonstration lesson.

Simulated model of a microcomputer keyboard.

Books: Frederick, Franz. *Guide to Microcomputers.*
The Pet Personal Computer Guide.

Introductory computer software such as *Apple Presents Apple.*

Software resources (see page 251).

Methods:

The teacher will:
1. Work with the library media specialist to plan and prepare a video taped demonstration lesson to help students identify and use the various parts of a microcomputer. The following parts should be labeled: Input, Central Processing Unit, Output, Memory, Arithmetic Unit.
2. Schedule the playback of the video taped demonstration lesson.
3. Schedule students in groups of two to visit the computer center to use the microcomputers.

The library media specialist will:
1. Assist with planning the demonstration lesson.
2. Videotape the demonstration lesson.
3. Prepare simulated microcomputer keyboards on cardboard for students to use while viewing the demonstration lesson.
4. Supervise the computer center.

Methods (cont'd.)

The students will:

1. View the video taped demonstration lesson.

2. Use the simulated microcomputer keyboard.

3. Identify the parts of the microcomputer.

4. Use the microcomputer to catalog a diskette, and load, run, break out, and rerun a program.

Evaluative Criteria: The students will successfully identify the parts of a microcomputer and will use the microcomputer to perform basic tasks.

LESSON 24 / 103

LESSON 24

Title: Dinosaurs Revisited.

Overview: The purpose of this lesson is to utilize a filmstrip and an audiocard system to provide information on dinosaurs for students with special needs.

Library Media Skills Objectives:

Find out specific information using a filmstrip.

Use an audiocard machine.

Performance Objective: Given a filmstrip and an audiocard program on dinosaurs, the students will identify scientific names and descriptions of at least five dinosaurs.

Subject Area: Science.

Learning Strategy: Audiovisual instruction, discussion.

Resources:

Filmstrip: *Dinosaurs.* National Geographic Society.

Audiocard Program: *How to Speak Dinosaur: A Look at Prehistoric Animals.* Audiotronics.

Methods:

The teacher will:
1. Introduce the lesson by writing vocabulary words on the chalkboard: dinosaurs, fossils, paleontologist.
2. Tell the students that they are going to the library media center to see a filmstrip on dinosaurs and to use the audiocard readers to learn the names of some dinosaurs.
3. Schedule class with library media specialist.
4. Check student responses on audiocard.
5. Plan a field trip to a museum to view exhibits of fossils.

The library media specialist will:
1. Show the filmstrip *Dinosaurs.*
2. Discuss the filmstrip with students.
3. Assist students with audiocard machines.
4. Display books of dinosaurs and prehistoric mammals and birds.

The students will:
1. View filmstrip.
2. Discuss the world in which dinosaurs lived.
3. Use audiocards to record responses giving scientific names and descriptions of dinosaurs.

Methods (cont'd.)

4. Do such optional activities as
    - check out a book on dinosaurs.
    - draw pictures of dinosaurs.
    - make clay models of dinosaurs.
    - record a story about dinosaurs.

Evaluative Criteria: The students will correctly identify scientific names and descriptions of at least five dinosaurs.

LESSON 25

Title: Pick Your Own!

Overview: The purpose of this lesson is to allow students to select fiction books of their choice for use in reading class. All books must be from the library media center or on the approved list. The students will have a conference with the teacher to discuss each book.

Library Media Skills Objectives:

Recognize different types of fiction books.

Define and identify in fictional works:
    plot, character, setting, theme.

Select reading material relevant to interests and purposes.

Performance Objective: Given guidelines for self-selection of fiction books, the students will select and read at least three fiction books each grading period and will have a conference with the teacher to discuss each book.

Subject Area: Reading.

Learning Strategy: Reading, discussion.

Resources:

Fiction collection.

Books on reading guidance: Carlson, G. Robert. *Books and the Teen-Age Reader.* rev. ed.
                            Books for the Teen Age, 1982 Annual.

Bibliographies: *Newbery Award Books.*
                   Books for Today's Young Readers: An Annotated Bibliography of Recommended Fiction for Ages 10-14.
                   Books for the Gifted Child.

Fiction: Self-Selection Guidelines (see page 106).

Book talks.

Methods:

The teacher will:
1. Plan with the library media specialist for students to come to the library media center from reading class to select books.
2. Explain the objective.
3. Discuss the literary analysis skills that will be used during the conference period: setting, characters, plot, conflict, theme, style.
4. Encourage students to read many different types of fiction books: science fiction, fantasy, historical fiction, humor, mystery and detective.

Fiction: Self-Selection Guidelines

All fiction books are arranged on the shelves alphabetically by the first two letters of the author's last name:

Alexander, Lloyd. *Westmark.*   F Al

Blume, Judy. *Tiger Eyes.*   F Bl

Childers, Alice. *Rainbow Jordan*   F Ch

1. Look for books by your favorite author.

2. Look at Fiction Chart. Many books have these labels on the spines.

SPORTS

FANTASY

MYSTERY AND DETECTIVE

ANIMAL STORIES

3. Browse: look at cover, blurb on book jacket.

4. Look at displays in the library media center.

5. Check author, title, and subject heading in card catalog.

6. Use bibliographies in reading textbook.

7. Use these books:
    Joy of Reading.
    Hooked on Books.
    Books and the Teen-Age Reader.
    Books for the Teen Age, 1982 Annual.

8. Ask for suggestions from:
    a friend, your reading teacher, your library media specialist.

9. Use bibliographies: *Newbery Award Books.*
    Books for Today's Young Readers: An Annotated Bibliography of Recommended Fiction for Ages 10-14.

Methods (cont'd.)

The library media specialist will:

1. Develop an up-to-date, comprehensive fiction collection.
2. Read as many fiction books as possible from the collection.
3. Make attractive displays of fiction books.
4. Use labels on spines of fiction books (see page 108).
5. Make a Fiction Chart displaying labels.
6. Give reading guidance as needed.
7. Give book talks.
8. Assist teacher with conferences.

The students will:

1. Use self-selection guidelines.
2. Select books.
3. Read books.
4. Plan for conferences with teacher.
   Review: setting, characters, plot, conflict, theme, style.
5. Visit public library and bookstores for additional selections. (optional)

Evaluative Criteria: The students will select and read at least three fiction books each grading period and will have a conference with the teacher to discuss each book.

Label for Science Fiction Books

7

Skills Lessons for Grade Seven

LESSON 1

Title: Dewey Jackpot.

Overview: The purpose of this lesson is to assist students in learning the ten main classes and some important divisions of the Dewey Decimal Classification System to help them locate books.

Library Media Skills Objectives:

Use Dewey Decimal Classification System.

Performance Objective: Given a review of the ten main classes and some important divisions of the Dewey Decimal Classification System, the students will play Dewey Jackpot for prizes.

Subject Area: Reading.

Learning Strategy: Game.

Resources:

35 Jackpot cards for Main Classes (see page 110).

35 Jackpot cards for Divisions (see page 110).

2 Master cards for Main Classes. (Cut up one to use for call numbers.) (See page 110.)

Call numbers for Main Classes.

2 Master cards for Divisions. (Cut up one to use for call numbers.) (See page 110.)

Call numbers for Divisions.

Study Guides (see page 111).

Prizes: Bookmarks, media center buttons, paperback books.

(Text continues on page 112.)

Samples of Jackpot Cards
MAIN CLASS

J	A	C	K	P	O	T
100	900	700	3C0	200	800	000
900	300	500	600	400	300	100
300	400	900	700	500	200	900
700	700	000	500	900	900	800
500	200	100	200	700	800	100
600	100	800	800	000	700	300
400	000	300	900	300	100	400

Make each card different with random selection of numbers

SELECTED DIVISION

J	A	C	K	P	O	T
	790			510		970
			530			
	920			921		380

Partial Sample

MASTER CARD — MAIN CLASS

J	A	C	K	P	O	T
000	000	000	000	000	000	000
100	100	100	100	100	100	100
200						
300						

Partial Sample

MASTER CARD — SELECTED DIVISION

550	920	350	970	620	590	510
280	790					

Partial Sample

MASTER FOR DEWEY CHIPS

DEWEY	DEWEY	DEWEY	DEWEY	DEWEY	

Partial Sample

Study Guide
Dewey Decimal Classification System
Main Classes

000	Generalities
100	Philosophy
200	Religion
300	The Social Sciences
400	Language
500	Pure Sciences
600	Technology (Applied Sciences)
700	The Arts
800	Literature
900	History

Important Divisions

030	General Encyclopedias
290	Comparative Religions
430	Germanic Languages
440	French Languages
460	Spanish Languages
510	Mathematics
520	Earth Sciences
580	Botanical Sciences
590	Zoological Sciences
610	Medical Sciences
620	Engineering
770	Photography
780	Music
790	Recreation
810	American Literature
820	English Literature
910	General Geography
920	General Biography
940	General History of Modern Europe
970	General History of North America

Resources (cont'd.)

Dewey Decimal Classification and Relative Index.

Sources for additional practice:

Dewey Dotto I, Dewey Dotto II. Larlin Corp.

Margrabe, Mary. *The "Now" Library: A Station's Approach Media Center Teaching Kit.*

Wieckert, Jeanne, and Irene Bell. *Media/Classroom Skills Games for the Middle School.* Vols. 1 and 2.

Methods:

The teacher will:

1. Plan the unit with the library media specialist who will have the primary responsibility for teaching the lesson.
2. Schedule the classes in the library media center.
3. Assist the library media specialist as a monitor and scorekeeper for the game.

The library media specialist will:

1. Prepare and laminate game cards, chips, and call numbers.
2. Review the Dewey Decimal Classification System with students.
3. Give each student a study guide.
4. Ask students to learn the information on the study guide for a Dewey Jackpot game the following class period.
5. Give out Jackpot Cards for Main Classes.
   Select call numbers as: K-300, A-900.
   Say "K-Social Science," "A-History."
6. Ask students to call out "Jackpot" when they have completed a horizontal, vertical, or diagonal sequence.
7. Have the teacher keep scores for students.
8. Switch, after a number of winners, to the Jackpot Cards for Selected Divisions.
9. Select call numbers as: T-510, K-970.
   Say "T-Mathematics," "K-General History of North America."
10. Total scores. Give students with 1 winner a bookmark, 2-4 winners a library media center button, 5 or more winners a paperback book.

The students will:

1. Review the ten main classes of the Dewey Decimal Classification System.
2. Learn selected divisions of the decimal classifications.
3. Play Dewey Jackpot.
4. Use main classes and divisions of the Dewey Decimal Classification System to locate books.

Evaluative Criteria: The students will play the Dewey Jackpot game and win prizes.

LESSON 2

Title: Wheels.

Overview: The purpose of this lesson is to provide students in remedial reading with a directed reading activity using a selected topic in magazines.

Library Media Skills Objectives:

Identify and locate magazines.

Locate topics using table of contents.

Skim to find relevant ideas.

Prepare a summary.

Performance Objective: Given the topic "Wheels," the students will locate and read an article in a magazine about one type of vehicle on wheels. They will complete a booklet that contains a cover with a picture, the title of the magazine, the title of the article, the type of wheeled vehicle, a list of vocabulary words, and a summary of the article.

Subject Area: Remedial Reading.

Learning Strategy: Discussion, reading, project.

Resources:

Magazines: *Bicycling.*
Car and Driver.
Car Craft.
Cycle.
Cycle World.
Hot Rod.
Motor Trend.

Methods:

The teacher will:

1. Introduce the lesson and objective.
2. Define purpose for reading.
3. Ask students to name vehicles that have wheels.
4. Discuss student responses.
5. State that many of the vehicles they have named are listed on cards as topics for reports.
6. Let students select one card from a box that contains cards with such topics as: motorcycles, automobiles, bicycles, mopeds, and racing automobiles.
7. Schedule students in the library media center for an introduction to magazines.
8. Work with individual students to develop vocabulary.
9. Reinforce skills for skimming, determining main idea, sequence of events, and summarizing.

Methods (cont'd.)

    10. Guide students in preparing a booklet.

    11. Evaluate booklet.

The library media specialist will:

    1. Locate magazines with articles on wheeled vehicles making certain to have magazines for each topic listed on the cards distributed by the teacher.

    2. Reserve magazines on a display rack in the magazine section of the library media center.

    3. Show the students the special rack of reserved magazines and allow them to select a magazine that might have information on their topic.

    4. Demonstrate the use of the table of contents to locate a topic in a magazine.

    5. Assist students in locating a magazine article on their topic.

    6. Allow students to check out the magazines.

    7. Give the teacher back copies of magazines that students can use to cut out pictures for the covers of their booklets.

The students will:

    1. Select a card from a box that contains cards with topics about wheeled vehicles.

    2. Select a magazine from the reserved collection in the library media center.

    3. Use the table of contents to locate an article on assigned topic.

    4. Check out the magazine from the library media center.

    5. Read the magazine article during class periods.

    6. Make a list of vocabulary words.

    7. Skim the article to find relevant ideas.

    8. Determine the main idea.

    9. List the sequence of events.

    10. Write a summary of the article.

    11. Prepare a booklet using the objectives as stated by the teacher.

Evaluative Criteria: The students will successfully complete a booklet that contains a cover with a picture of a wheeled vehicle, the titles of the magazine and the article that they used for their report, a list of vocabulary words, and a summary of the article.

LESSON 3

Title: Who Reads the Classics?

Overview: The purpose of this lesson is to have students select and read a novel from a selected list of the classics. They will read for enjoyment as well as to strengthen critical thinking skills. Three to five students may select the same novel. After the students complete the reading of the novel (the same novel), they will form a discussion group, complete an activity, and plan and produce a video tape based on the novel.

Library Media Skills Objectives:

Select and read a novel.

Identify the elements of a novel: theme(s), setting, plot, character traits, style.

Plan and produce a video tape.

Performance Objectives: Given specific information about the elements of a novel, a list of the classics, student activity sheets, a sample storyboard, and directions, the students will:

- Select and read a novel from the classics.
- Participate in small group discussions.
- Define *the classics.*
- Complete the Book Analysis Worksheet.
- Confer with the teacher.
- Plan a video tape production based on the novel read.
- Plot a storyboard and script.
- Prepare graphics.
- Rehearse scenes with library media specialist.
- Produce a video tape.
- Show production in class.
- Write an evaluation of production.

Subject Area: Language Arts.

Learning Strategy: Lecture, discussion, book talk, demonstration, audiovisual project.

Resources:

Novels from the classics (3 to 5 copies of each).

Suggestions: Alcott, Louisa M. *Little Women.*
DeFoe, Daniel. *Robinson Crusoe.*
Graham, Kenneth. *The Wind in the Willows.*
London, Jack. *The Call of the Wild.*
Rawlings, Marjorie. *The Yearling.*
Richter, Conrad. *The Light in the Forest.*
Steinbeck, John. *The Red Pony.*
Twain, Mark. *The Adventures of Tom Sawyer.*
Verne, Jules. *20,000 Leagues under the Sea.*

Resources (cont'd.)

Guidelines for Group Discussions (see page 117).

Book Analysis Worksheet (see page 118).

Sample Storyboard (see page 119).

Production Evaluation Worksheet (see page 120).

Methods:

The teacher will:

1. Introduce the lesson and discuss the objectives and evaluation criteria.
2. Review the elements of a novel: theme(s), setting, plot, character traits, style.
3. Discuss the Guidelines for Group Discussions.
4. Schedule activities in the library media center.
5. Confer with groups.
6. Grade Book Analysis Worksheet.

The library media specialist will:

1. Select and reserve novels from the classics.
2. Prepare a list of the novels.
3. Give a book talk on the classics.
4. Demonstrate storyboard techniques.
5. Show a sample video tape.
6. Assist with preparation of graphics.
7. Direct rehearsals.
8. Assist student crew with video tape production.
9. View and evaluate productions.
10. Grade group worksheet from Discussion Period III.

The students will:

1. Take notes on objectives and schedules.
2. Listen to book talk.
3. Read novels.
4. Complete worksheets.
5. Work with group using group guidelines.
6. View sample video tape.
7. Observe storyboard techniques.
8. Plot storyboard. Include background music.
9. Prepare graphics.
10. Assemble costumes and properties.
11. Videotape production.
12. View class productions and evaluate them using production evaluation worksheet.

(Text continues on page 120.)

Guidelines for Group Discussions

Name _____

Group Number_____

Period _____

Date _____

Directions: After reading the novel, select a leader of your group to guide the discussion periods and a recorder to list the major ideas discussed.

Discussion Period I:

Overview of the novel: Briefly summarize the novel by stating the beginning, middle, and end of the novel.

Each person should contribute ideas.

Discussion Period II:

Discuss each part of the Book Analysis Worksheet. You may use your books to verify your answers. Choose the best answers for the recorder to write on your worksheet. Turn in your group worksheet to your teacher for a letter grade.

Discussion Period III:

Review and recall comments, ideas, and the book talks on the classics. Define what is meant by *the classics.* You may use dictionaries and literary reference books and materials in the library media center. Answer the following question: Why do you think that the novel your group read is considered a classic? Record your group answer and turn it in to the library media specialist for a letter grade.

Discussion Period IV:

Brainstorm with your group to choose a scene from your novel to dramatize for your video tape production. You may want to read some selections aloud and to do some role-playing. Remember to use your imagination!

Book Analysis Worksheet

Name _____

Group Number _____

Period _____

Date _____

Title _____ Author _____

Publisher _____ Copyright _____

Directions: As a group, complete the following outline using your book:

Setting: Time _____

Place _____

Theme(s) _____

_____

Identify the main characters explaining what kind of person each character was.

1. _____

_____

2. _____

_____

3. _____

_____

Sample Storyboard

Production Evaluation Worksheet

Name _____

Group Number _____

Period _____

Date _____

Directions: The library media specialist will explain the evaluation criteria listed below. As you view each production, list the title then give it a rating in each box.

Production	Originality	Graphics and Titles	Technical Quality of Picture	Technical Quality of Sound	General Effectiveness
Example: 1. Treasure Island	3	2	3	3	3
2.					
3.					
4.					
5.					
6.					
7.					

1=Poor   2=Fair   3=Good   4=Excellent

Evaluative Criteria: The students will read a classic novel and follow directions and successfully complete all activities. The teacher and library media specialist will jointly evaluate the students' work including the student activity sheets that received a letter grade.

Special Note: This lesson can be adapted for students reading below grade level by using the comic book kit version of *Illustrated Classics* by Pendulum Press, Inc. Activities can be modified according to ability level. Students can make a video tape based on the *Illustrated Classics*.

LESSON 4

Title: Read All about It!

Overview: The purpose of this unit is to allow students to use the newspaper format to report events of the 1920s. The students will study about the *twenties* and will locate information to be used as news items.

Library Media Skills Objectives:

Identify the components of a newspaper.

Skim to find relevant material.

Organize information around a topic.

Produce a media presentation that contains specific subject matter.

Performance Objective: Given background information on the components of a newspaper and the period of history of the 1920s, the students will locate information and compose a newspaper about the 1920s.

Subject Area: Social Studies.

Learning Strategy: Lecture, discussion, practice, project.

Resources:

Newspapers.

Books: *The American Heritage History of the 20's and 30's.*
          Perett, Geoffrey. *America in the Twenties.*
          This Fabulous Century: 1920-1930. Time-Life.
          Gilbert, Nan. *See Yourself in Print.*
          Severn, William. *50 Ways to Have Fun with Old Newspapers.*

Methods:

The teacher will:

1.   Involve students in a study of events of the 1920s.
2.   Explain the objectives of the unit: to gather news items on the 1920s and to produce a newspaper.
3.   Invite the library media specialist to come to the classroom to give a lecture on the components of a newspaper.
4.   Schedule classes in the library media center for research.
5.   Choose an editor, reporters, artist, and proofreader.
6.   Type and duplicate the newspaper.
7.   Review and evaluate the newspaper with the class and the library media specialist.

Methods (cont'd.)

The library media specialist will:

1. Give a lecture on the components of a newspaper.

   Make large charts on tagboard to show the components of a newspaper:
   Front Page, Editorials, Business, Local News, World News, Entertainment, Obituaries, Advertisements.

2. Show books relating to the 1920s and clothes and artifacts from the 1920s.

3. Assist students with research on the twenties.

4. Help students with layout of news items for their newspaper on the 1920s.

5. Review and evaluate the newspaper.

The students will:

1. Learn the components of a newspaper.

2. Locate information on the 1920s: clothing styles, international events, entertainment, food fads, music, business news, local news, advertisements, people in the news, weather phenomena, life-styles.

3. Write articles for newspaper according to assignment: editor, international reporter, artist, etc.

4. Check layout of newspaper with library media specialist.

5. Give completed newspaper to teacher for typing and duplication.

6. Read and evaluate the newspaper.

Evaluative Criteria: The students will produce a newspaper reporting events of the 1920s.

LESSON 5

Title: For Novel Lovers.

Overview: The purpose of this lesson is to allow students to select a paperback book to read for pleasure. The students will evaluate the book on a card for the media center's reading guidance file, "Paperbacks, to Read or Not to Read."

Library Media Skills Objectives:

Select reading as a leisure-time activity.

Performance Objectives: Given a book talk featuring paperback novels and a reading guidance card, the students will select and read a paperback novel of their choice. They will successfully complete the reading guidance card by evaluating the book.

Subject Area: Reading.

Learning Strategy: Book talk, reading.

Resources:

Blume, Judy. *Deenie.*
  It's Not the End of the World.

Byars, Betsy. *The Pinballs.*

Cavanna, Betty. *You Can't Take Twenty Dogs on a Date.*

Colman, Hila. *Sometimes I Don't Love My Mother.*

Conford, Ellen. *Dear Lovey Hart, I Am Desperate.*

Daly, Maureen. *Seventeenth Summer.*

Danzier, Paula. *The Pistachio Prescription.*

Gathje, Curtis. *The Disco Kid.*

Girion, Barbara. *Like Everybody Else.*

Greene, Bette. *The Summer of My German Soldier.*

Hinton, S. E. *The Outsiders.*

Kerr, M. E. *Gentlehands.*

Knudson, R. R. *Zanboomer.*

L'Engle, Madeleine. *The Moon by Night.*

Lyle, Katie. *I Will Go Barefoot All Summer for You.*

Miles, Betty. *The Trouble with Thirteen.*

Paterson, Katherine. *Jacob Have I Loved.*

Resources (cont'd.)

Peck, Richard. *Close Enough to Touch.*

Pevsner, Stella. *Cute Is a Four Letter Word.*

Platt, Kim.   *Run for Your Life.*

Rodowsky, Colby. *What about Me?*

Sachs, Marilyn. *Class Pictures.*

Wood, Phyllis. *This Time Count Me In.*

Zindel, Paul.   *Girl Who Wanted a Boy.*

Sample Reading Guidance card.

Reading Guidance Card

Author _____

Title _____

Brief Summary _____

_____

Recommended   ☐

Not Recommended ☐

Methods:

The teacher will:

1.   Introduce the lesson.
2.   Schedule the book talk with the library media specialist.
3.   Accompany the class to the media center for the book talk.
4.   Read and review reading guidance cards with the library media specialist.

The library media specialist will:

1.   Select and purchase a variety of paperback books following the approved selection policy.
2.   Read many paperback novels.
3.   Select paperbacks and prepare book talk.
4.   Present a lively, exciting book talk.
5.   Show students a sample reading guidance card.

Methods (cont'd.)

6. Ask students to complete the card after they have read a paperback book. Tell them that the cards will be reviewed by the teacher and library media specialist and that selected cards of general interest will be included in the card file, "Paperbacks, to Read or Not to Read."

7. Place a sign in the media center next to a 4" x 6" card file that states:

    Paperbacks, to Read or Not to Read
    Compiled by Students for Students

8. Review reading guidance cards and evaluate with reading teacher.

9. Select cards to be included in the card file in the media center.

The students will:

1. Listen to book talk.

2. Select and read a paperback novel.

3. Complete reading guidance card.

Evaluative Criteria: The students will select and read a paperback novel and correctly complete a reading guidance card.

LESSON 6

Title: News Quiz.

Overview: The purpose of this activity is to stimulate students to learn about current events by reading news magazines. They will compete in a news quiz contest that will be presented to their classes on closed-circuit television.

Library Media Skills Objectives:

Select periodicals for current information.

Find specific information using headings and subheadings.

Skim materials to find answers in resources.

Operate video tape equipment.

Performance Objective: Given current issues of *Time, Newsweek, U. S. News and World Report* magazines and a list of questions, selected students will compete in a news quiz game.

Subject Area: Social Studies.

Learning Strategy: Game.

Resources:

The Weekly News Quiz Game.
    Creative Educational Services
    P. O. Box 30501
    Santa Barbara, CA 93105

Magazines: *Time, Newsweek, U. S. News and World Report.*

Production Notes (see page 127).

News Quiz Script (see page 128).

Score Card (see page 129).

Methods:

The teacher will:

1. Review the questions and answers from *The Weekly News Quiz Game.* Select questions to be asked of students.

2. Prepare a study guide for students by including some of the questions on the News Quiz. Examples are:
   • Who is the Chancellor of West Germany?
   • What country is the largest importer of grain?
   • What is the favorite charity of Nancy Reagan?

(Text continues on page 130.)

Production Notes

News Quiz

MEDIA TECHS:

Director. . . . . .Bobby Smith
Engineer . . . . .Tyrone Black
Music. . . . . .David Zens
Sound . . . . James Gibbs
Visuals (Signs). . . . . Scott Thomas
Cameras. . . . . .Pat Long
                                        Jean Love

1. SET UP EQUIPMENT:

   Check focus on camera.

   Check visuals for alignment on camera.

   Check RF Converter—"ON."

   Check channel 8 on TV in media center for picture and sound.

   Have sound person turn on sound on lectern and check mike and sound on TV recorder.

   Check student lights.

2. BEFORE BEGINNING:

   Check to see all contestants in place.

   Scorekeeper, timekeeper, and judge in place.

   Ask Mrs. Manning if she is ready.

3. BEGIN MUSIC.

   Switcher is on Camera 2.

   H.M.S.
   T.V.
   8

   Change signs.

   BIWEEKLY
   NEWS QUIZ

   Turn music off.

   Switch to Camera 1 on Mrs. Manning.

4. FILM TO END OF ROUND 1. Turn up music. Pan camera to pictures of contestants. When score visual is in place, turn down music and switch to Camera 2. Switch back to Camera 1 for Round 2.

5. REPEAT NO. 4 at end of Round 2 and Round 3.

6. AT END OF PROGRAM turn up music. Pan Camera.

News Quiz Script

MUSIC	HMS TV 8 Sign
MUSIC	BIWEEKLY NEWS QUIZ SHOW
ANCHORPERSON	Welcome to our Biweekly News Quiz Show.
	Our panels will introduce themselves.
PANEL 1	(Introduction)
PANEL 2	(Introduction)
ANCHORPERSON	Each question must be answered within ten seconds. After conferring with team members the first captain *to signal will immediately answer the question.* If the answer is incorrect the team loses five points and the opposite team may answer.
	Round 1 will be fifteen minutes long. Each question will be worth 5 points.
	Round 2 will be eight minutes long. Each question will be worth 10 points.
	Round 3 will be five minutes long. Each question will be worth 15 points.
	The score will be given after each round.
	All decisions by the judge are final.
	The judge is _____ .
	The scorekeeper is _____ .
	The timekeeper is _____ .

Score Card Sample	PANEL 1	PANEL 2
ROUND 1	5 5 5 5 5 5 5 5 5 5 5 5 5 5 5 5 5 5 5 5 5 5 5 5 5 5 5 5 5 5 -5 -5 -5 -5 -5 -5 -5 -5 -5 -5 -5 -5	5 5 5 5 5 5 5 5 5 5 5 5 5 5 5 5 5 5 5 5 5 5 5 5 5 5 5 5 5 5 -5 -5 -5 -5 -5 -5 -5 -5 -5 -5 -5 -5
5 Points	Round 1 Total A = 55	Round 1 Total A = 25
ROUND 2	10 10 10 10 10 10 10 10 10 10 10 10 10 10 10 10 10 10 10 10 -5 -5 -5 -5 -5 -5	10 10 10 10 10 10 10 10 10 10 10 10 10 10 10 10 10 10 10 10 -5 -5 -5 -5 -5 -5
10 Points	Round 2 Total A+B=C B = 75 C = 130	Round 2 Total A+B=C B = 60 C = 85
Round 3	15 15 15 15 15 15 15 15 15 15 15 15 15 15 15 15 15 15 15 15 -5 -5 -5 -5	15 15 15 15 15 15 15 15 15 15 15 15 15 15 15 15 15 15 15 15 -5 -5 -5 -5
15 Points	Round 3 Total C+D= D = 55 185	Round 3 Total C+D= D. = 85 170

Methods (cont'd.)

3.　In large group session, let students select two panels of contestants. Each panel will have four members. Appoint a judge, time keeper, and scorekeeper.

4.　Serve as anchorperson on news quiz show.

The library media specialist will:

1.　Order *The Weekly News Quiz Game* and magazines.

2.　Train student assistants to produce closed-circuit television.

3.　Set up studio for news quiz show:

　　a.　Use sound system with microphone for anchorperson.

　　b.　Set up two long tables with four chairs and a buzzer or light switch for student contestants to activate.

4.　Set up tables for scorekeeper, timekeeper and judge.

5.　Prepare signs.

6.　Select production crew.

7.　Supervise production.

The students will:

1.　Read magazines.

2.　Locate answers to questions.

3.　Serve as panelists on News Quiz Show.

4.　Produce the News Quiz Show.

Evaluative Criteria: The students will compete as panelists on the News Quiz Show or will successfully produce the show on closed-circuit television.

LESSON 7

Title: Here's to Health!

Overview: The purpose of this lesson is to provide students with the necessary skills to effectively research and prepare a written report on a disease. It is a part of a health unit where students will compare and contrast communicable and noncommunicable diseases.

Library Media Skills Objectives:

Locate material using an index, the card catalog, the vertical file, *Readers' Guide to Periodical Literature.*

Select material based on usefulness, appropriateness, and accuracy.

Interpret information.

Identify the main idea.

Prepare notes, an outline, and a bibliography.

Performance Objective: Given report guidelines, the students will locate information on a disease, take notes on cards, write a well-organized, concise report, and prepare a bibliography. The note cards will be turned in with the report.

Subject Area: Health.

Learning Strategy: Lecture, demonstration, individual project.

Resources:

Books: Donahue, Parnell. *Germs Make Me Sick.*
Nourse, Alan. *Lumps, Bumps, and Rashes.*
Newman, Gerald. *The Encyclopedia of Health and the Human Body.*
Silverstein, Alvin, and Virginia Silverstein. *Itch, Sniffle and Sneeze.*
Tully, Marianne, and Mary Alice Tully. *Dread Diseases.*

Magazines: *Family Health.*

Filmstrips: *Good Health Series.* Marsh Films.

Sample Note Card (see page 132).

Transparencies of a sample report (including note cards, outline, and bibliography).

Report Guidelines (see page 132).

Methods:

The teacher will:

1.   Suggest topics for disease reports.
2.   Suggest subtopics: symptoms, modes of transmission, prevention, treatment.
3.   Schedule classes in the library media center.

Sample Note Card

Cancer   Source: Haines, Gail. *Cancer.* New York: Franklin Watts, 1980.

Causes: chemicals, radiation, viruses.

Symptoms: nagging cough, nonhealing sore, lump.

Report Guidelines

WRITING A RESEARCH PAPER ON DISEASES

Objective: The student will write a well-organized, concise report on a disease and include a bibliography showing the sources of information. The student will use the following steps in preparing the report:

1. Determine the topic.

2. Locate information.

3. Skim information.

4. Make an outline of subtopics.

5. Take notes on cards. Include bibliographic information on cards.

6. Write report.

7. Make bibliography.

8. Turn in note cards with the report.

Methods (cont'd.)

4.   Assist students with research.

5.   Grade disease reports.

The library media specialist will:

1.   Review location and use of media resources including the *Readers' Guide to Periodical Literature.*

2.   Discuss note taking, outlining, and summarizing.

3.   Demonstrate study skill procedures by showing transparencies of a completed disease report with note cards, outline, and bibliography.

4.   Read sample report to class.

5.   Assist individual students as necessary.

6.   Read and evaluate completed reports.

The students will:

1.   Attend lecture.

2.   Review note taking, outlining, and summarizing.

3.   Observe demonstration of sample report.

4.   Locate source material, prepare note cards and outline, write report, compile bibliography.

Evaluative Criteria: The student will follow all directions correctly and will submit a research paper on a disease.

LESSON 8

Title: Searching for Answers.

Overview: The purpose of this lesson is to challenge highly able readers to determine the order of arrangement of entries in reference books and nonprint materials. They will differentiate between alphabetical order, calendar order, chronological order, geographical order, and numerical order.

Library Media Skills Objectives:

Identify: alphabetical order, calendar order, chronological order, geographical order, and numerical order.

Performance Objective: Given a worksheet, the students will answer questions giving the definition and at least three examples of alphabetical order, calendar order, chronological order, geographical order, and numerical order.

Subject Area: Reading.

Learning Strategy: Practice.

Resources:

Card catalog.

Books:

World Almanac.
American Book of Days.
People in Books.
Webster's Guide to American History.
Atlas of Man.
Current Biography.
Rand McNally Cosmopolitan World Atlas.
Encyclopaedia Britannica.
Guinness Book of World Records.
Occupational Outlook Handbook.
Famous First Facts.
Familiar Quotations.
Almanac of Dates.

Computer software.

Microfiche.

Card file.

Reference section.

Vertical file.

Worksheet.

Worksheet: Searching for Answers

When you use an index, you know that it is often arranged in alphabetical order. What do you know about other methods of arranging materials in resources? Here is a list of a few types of orders:

> Alphabetical order
> Calendar order
> Chronological order
> Geographical order
> Numerical order

Can you add other types?

Define each type of order and locate at least three reference sources that use these orders.

Alphabetical order: _____

_____

    Reference sources: _____

_____

Calendar order: _____

_____

    Reference sources: _____

_____

Chronological order: _____

_____

    Reference sources: _____

_____

Geographical order: _____

_____

    Reference sources: _____

_____

Numerical order: _____

_____

    Reference sources: _____

_____

Others: _____

_____

(Note: Reference sources may include the card catalog, indexes, and nonprint materials.)

Methods:

The teacher will:

1. Discuss the lesson with the library media specialist who will have the primary responsibility for teaching the lesson.

2. Schedule classes in the library media center.

3. Reinforce concepts in class, when applicable.

The library media specialist will:

1. Prepare a worksheet.

2. Check resources and complete a worksheet to use with students after they have completed the assignment.

3. Check worksheets as students complete assignment.

4. Show resources to students, if necessary.

The students will:

1. Define alphabetical order, calendar order, chronological order, geographical order, and numerical order.

2. Search resources of library media center to locate examples of types of order.

3. Evaluate worksheet with the library media specialist.

Evaluative Criteria: The students will successfully complete the worksheet defining types of order with at least three examples of alphabetical order, calendar order, chronological order, geographical order, and numerical order.

LESSON 9

Title: Unaccustomed as I Am to Public Speaking.

Overview: The purpose of this unit is to provide students with the opportunity to develop their public speaking ability by planning, presenting, recording on video tape, viewing, and evaluating a speech.

Library Media Skills Objectives:

Select resources using the card catalog.

Select reference sources to find information on a given subject.

Select periodicals and newspapers for current information.

Summarize information found in resources.

Use note-taking skills.

Organize information.

Operate a microform viewer.

Prepare a video tape.

Performance Objectives: Given specific information on preparing a speech, the students will select a topic and utilize reference sources to successfully write and present a speech on video tape. They will view and evaluate their speech.

Subject Area: Reading.

Learning Strategy: Lecture, demonstration, practice, audiovisual project.

Resources:

Books: Powers, David. *How to Make a Speech.*
Gilford, Henry. *How to Give a Speech.*
Prochnou, Herbert. *The Toastmaster's Handbook.*

Video tape of student speeches from previous year.

Microfiche catalog for interlibrary loan.

Guidelines for making a storyboard (see page 119).

Bibliographic guidelines.

Methods:

The teacher will:

1. Present information on effective public speaking techniques.
2. Suggest topics for speeches.
3. Define objectives and evaluative criteria.

Methods (cont'd.)

4. Schedule reference and video tape sessions with the library media specialist.
5. Grade written report and video tape presentation.

The library media specialist will:

1. Demonstrate use of reference sources.
2. Show video tape example of student speeches from previous year.
3. Demonstrate use of microfiche reader.
4. Explain use of interlibrary loan of material.
5. Obtain resources from other libraries.
6. Assist with research.
7. Demonstrate storyboard techniques.
8. Assist with video tape production.
9. Evaluate unit.

The student will:

1. Select a topic.
2. Locate and utilize resources.
3. Take notes, summarize information, prepare written report, prepare bibliography.
4. Plan and present speech on video tape using at least one visual aid.
5. View and evaluate speeches.

Evaluative Criteria: The students will follow directions to successfully prepare a written report and an oral presentation on a topic of their choice.

LESSON 10

Title: To Buy or Not to Buy.

Overview: The purpose of this lesson is to introduce the magazines *Consumer Reports* and *Penny Power* to provide students with sources of information on comparative shopping.

Library Media Skills Objectives:

Use table of contents of magazines to locate articles.

Interpret specialized reference materials to select data bearing on a problem.

Draw appropriate conclusions based on information presented.

Distinguish between fact and opinion.

Performance Objective: Given background information and copies of *Consumer Reports* and *Penny Power* magazines, the students will give the name of the magazines, tell the purpose of the magazines, interpret the ratings, and draw appropriate conclusions based on information presented.

Subject Area: Social Studies.

Learning Strategy: Large group presentation, practice.

Resources:

Classroom sets of *Consumer Reports* and *Penny Power* magazines.

Worksheet (see page 140).

Newspaper ads.

Magazine ads.

Television ads.

Products for taste test: cola, potato chips, peanut butter.

Transparencies: Think Before You Spend, sample ads from various media, "The Claims and the Facts." *Penny Power* (December/January 1983): 5.

Taste test ballots (see page 140).

Methods:

The teacher will:
1. Jointly plan the unit with the library media specialist and designate responsibilities.
2. Purchase products for taste test.
3. Schedule large group meeting of class.
4. Participate in disucssion led by the library media specialist.
5. Tabulate scores from taste test.
6. Present follow-up lesson in class by distributing worksheets and copies of *Consumer Reports* and *Penny Power* magazines.

Worksheet: To Buy or Not to Buy

1. The title of the magazine that is a *special consumer magazine* for young people is
   _____

   Read an article. List title of article _____

2. The purpose of *Consumer Reports* magazine is_____

   _____

3. How are products obtained for testing?_____

   _____

4. Use the table of contents of *Consumer Reports* to locate an article of interest to you. Answer the following questions:

   Date of issue of magazine _____

   Title of article_____

   Name of product_____

   Skim and summarize background information about the product _____

   _____

   _____

   List terms used in ratings_____

   _____

   Is a "best buy" designated?_____

   Conclusions about products. Are they based on fact or opinion?_____

   _____

Sample Taste Test Ballot

(Choose product you like best.)

	BRAND
COLA	A B C
PEANUT BUTTER	A B C
POTATO CHIPS	A B C

Methods (cont'd.)

The library media specialist will:

1. Prepare a large group presentation.
   - Have transparency "THINK BEFORE YOU SPEND" on overhead and play a lively record while students are being seated.
   - Ask the question, "If you want to purchase a product, where do you get information that helps you to make a wise choice?"
   - Show sample newspaper ads, magazine ads, and a television commercial. Use commercial made by students, if possible. Examples could be a "Fizzle Cola" or "Bubblemania" commercial.
   - Show a transparency of page 5 of *Penny Power* (December/January 1983), "The Claims and the Facts." State "Two magazines produced by Consumers Union provide shoppers with information on comparative shopping: *Consumer Reports* and *Penny Power.*"
   - Give background information on Consumers Union, laboratory tests, and ratings.
   - Present information on "Fast Foods" (*Consumer Reports,* May 1975, September 1979); "Low Cost Stereo Receivers" (*Consumer Reports*, June 1983); "Arcade Fever" (*Penny Power*, December/January 1983).
2. Ask students to participate in a taste test judging: appearance, smell, texture, taste.
3. Hand out ballots. Ask students to circle the best brand.
4. Tabulate scores on chalkboard.
5. Reveal brand names for each product, e.g.,
   A: Coca Cola.
   B: Pepsi Cola.
   C: Giant Cola.
6. Evaluate lesson with teacher after students complete worksheet in class.

The students will:

1. Participate in large group instruction.
2. Take taste test.
3. Complete worksheet in classroom.

Evaluative Criteria: The students will use *Consumer Reports* and *Penny Power* magazines to successfully complete the worksheet.

LESSON 11

Title: Budding Scientists.

Overview: The purpose of this lesson is to introduce the *Peterson Field Guide Series* to students to assist them with identification and classification of birds, trees, insects, shells, butterflies, and wildflowers.

Library Media Skills Objectives:

Interpret specialized reference materials to select data bearing on a problem.

Select sources based upon their authority, usefulness, appropriateness.

Performance Objectives: Given a learning center activity with books from *Peterson Field Guide Series,* the students will determine the author and publisher, interpret the data, and use the book to identify a series of pictures of birds, trees, etc.

Subject Area: Science.

Learning Strategy: Learning Center.

Resources:

Learning centers with collections of pictures of shells, butterflies, insects, trees, birds, and wild-flowers (these could be slides, pictures from magazines, or photographs made from books).

Books: *Peterson Field Guide Series:*
1. *A Field Guide to Birds.*
2. *A Field Guide to Shells.*
3. *A Field Guide to Butterflies.*
4. *A Field Guide to Trees and Shrubs.*
5. *A Field Guide to Insects.*
6. *A Field Guide to Wildflowers of Northeastern and North-Central North America.*

Publications of National Audubon Society, National Wildlife Federation.

Methods:

The teacher will:
1. Discuss scientific methods of classification and identification.
2. Assist students at stations as they use field guides to identify collections of pictures.
3. Schedule activities in the library media center.
4. After stations are completed, discuss the scope, format, and authority of the *Peterson Field Guide Series.*

Methods (cont'd.)

The library media specialist will:

1. Set up seven learning centers, six of them with a collection of pictures and a corresponding book from the *Peterson Field Guide Series,* the seventh with information about the National Audubon Society, National Wildlife Federation, and Roger Tory Peterson. Examples of information might be:

> The National Audubon Society, founded in 1905, promotes conservation and protection of wildlife. It produces motion pictures for Audubon Wildlife Tours and publishes the Audubon Magazine.
>
> The National Wildlife Federation promotes conservation, protection, and restoration of forests and wildlife in the United States. It publishes *National Wildlife* and *Ranger Rick's Nature Magazine.*
>
> Roger Tory Peterson, born in 1908, is a well-known ornithologist, conservationist, artist, and author. He has received many awards, honors, and citations as a naturalist. His field guide series stimulated national interest in the environmental movement.

2. Make a worksheet for each station.

Worksheets

Station 1   BIRDS

Identify at least 10 birds by using *A Field Guide to Birds.*

List the letter from the top of the picture and give the name of the bird.

Example: 1. C   Baltimore Oriole

1.	4.	7.	10.
2.	5.	8.	11.
3.	6.	9.	12.

Station 7   National Audubon Society

National Wildlife Federation

Roger Tory Peterson

Look at the collection of magazines and the information on the above topics. List at least 5 facts that reflect the purpose, authority, or accomplishments of the National Audubon Society, National Wildlife Federation, or Roger Tory Peterson.

Methods (cont'd.)

The students will:

1. Complete at least three stations including Station 7.
2. Discuss the scope, format, and authority of the *Peterson Field Guide Series.*

Evaluative Criteria: The students will successfully complete at least three stations using the *Peterson Field Guide Series.*

LESSON 12

Title: What's Cooking?

Overview: The purpose of this unit is for students to locate information on foods and nutrition by using the card catalog, the Dewey Decimal Classification System, and *Readers' Guide to Periodical Literature.* The students will prepare a project utilizing the information from the resources in the library media center.

Library Media Skills Objectives:

Use the card catalog subject headings to locate resources.

Use the Dewey Decimal Classification System.

Use *Readers' Guide to Periodical Literature.*

Performance Objective: Given a list of nutrition topics, suggestions for food reports, and a review of library media reference skills, the students will select a nutrition topic, a food, or a food dish and use the resources in the library media center to find information on their topic. They will prepare and present a project to the class that may be a demonstration, written report, taped report, poster, or illustration.

Subject Area: Home Economics.

Learning Strategy: Lecture, discussion, project.

Resources:

Readers' Guide to Periodical Literature.

Magazines.

Transparencies: Subject Headings (see page 146).
Dewey Decimal Classification (see page 146).
Readers' Guide to Periodical Literature (see page 146).

Books: Burns, Marilyn. *Good for Me.*
Cooper, Terry. *Many Hands Cooking.*
Davis, Myrna. *The Potato Book.*
Gilbert, Sara. *You Are What You Eat.*
Lavine, Sigmund. *Indian Corn and Other Gifts.*
Oxford Book of Food Plants.
Perl, Lila. *Hunter's Stew and Hangtown Fry.*
Simon, Seymour. *About the Foods You Eat.*

Kits: *Food for the World.* National Geographic.
The Great Nutrition Robbery. Westinghouse Learning Corp.
What's Good to Eat: Foods the Body Needs. National Geographic.

Nutrition Topics and Suggestions for Food Reports (see page 147).

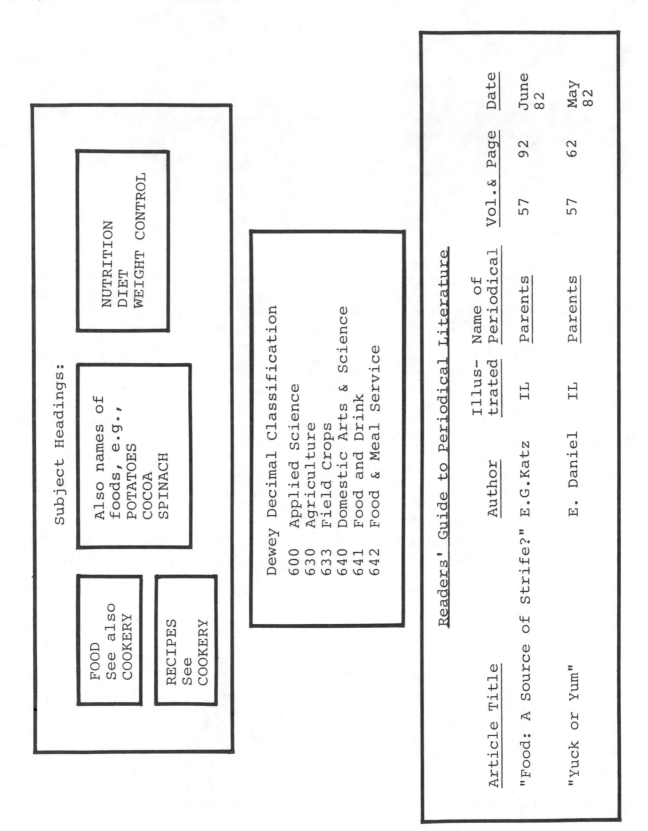

Subject Headings:

```
NUTRITION
DIET
WEIGHT CONTROL
```

```
Also names of
foods, e.g.,
POTATOES
COCOA
SPINACH
```

```
FOOD
See also
COOKERY
```

```
RECIPES
See
COOKERY
```

Dewey Decimal Classification

```
600  Applied Science
630  Agriculture
633  Field Crops
640  Domestic Arts & Science
641  Food and Drink
642  Food & Meal Service
```

Readers' Guide to Periodical Literature

Article Title	Author	Illus-trated	Name of Periodical	Vol.& Page	Date
"Food: A Source of Strife?"	E.G. Katz	IL	Parents	57 92	June 82
"Yuck or Yum"	E. Daniel	IL	Parents	57 62	May 82

Sample
Nutrition Topics

Food Additives	Vegetarians
Snacks	Basic Food Groups
Milk and Milk Products	Frozen Foods
Vitamins	Obesity and Nutrition
Fad Diets	

Suggestions for Food Reports

Common name	Recipes
Latin name or name of origin	Variation
Background information	Preparation
How food is used	Interesting facts

Methods:

The teacher will:

1. Plan the objectives and activities with the library media specialist.
2. Introduce the unit and discuss the objectives with the students.
3. Give students copies of suggested topics.
4. Schedule and accompany classes in the library media center.
5. Serve as a resource person to students.
6. Grade student projects.
7. Evaluate unit with library media specialist.

The library media specialist will:

1. Prepare and use transparencies to review subject headings, the Dewey Decimal Classification numbers for nutrition and food, and the *Readers' Guide to Periodical Literature.*
2. Assist students in locating magazine articles and other print and nonprint reference materials.
3. Assist students with preparation of graphics or audiovisual aids for projects.
4. Attend student presentations of projects.
5. Evaluate unit with teacher.

Methods (cont'd.)

The students will:

1. Select a topic.
2. Participate in review of library media skills.
3. Locate resources for topics by using the card catalog, the Dewey Decimal Classification System, and *Readers' Guide to Periodical Literature.*
4. Plan and prepare a project to present to the class.

Evaluative Criteria: The students will successfully locate information and prepare and present a project to the class on a nutrition topic, a food, or a food dish.

LESSON 13

Title: Be a Quiz Whiz.

Overview: The purpose of this activity is for students to learn about the accomplishments of famous black Americans by locating and utilizing information in resources in the library media center.

Library Media Skills Objectives:

Use special dictionaries.

Use an index of special reference sources.

Interpret information found in resources.

Performance Objective: Given a series of pictures of famous black Americans and a list of accomplishments, the students will use special reference sources to correctly match the two.

Subject Area: Social Studies.

Learning Strategy: Learning Center.

Resources:

Study Prints: *Famous Black Americans.* Audiovisual Enterprises.

Books: *Ebony Pictorial History of Black America.*
        Adams, Russell. *Great Negroes, Past and Present.*
        Bontemps, Arna. *Famous Negro Athletes.*

Worksheet (see page 150).

Methods:

The teacher will:
1. Permit individual or small groups of students to go to the library media center to complete the media quiz.
2. Display the winning entry in class area.

The library media specialist will:
1. Prepare an attractive display of pictures of famous black Americans at the media quiz center.
2. Prepare a worksheet.
3. Place special reference sources in the learning center.
4. Grade worksheet entries. Place all entries with the correct answers in a box. Draw one entry from the box. Post the name of the winner in the library media center. Return the winning entry to the teacher.
5. Award a prize to the winner.

The students will:
1. Use special reference sources to complete the following worksheet.

Worksheet
Famous Black Americans

_____ 1. Edward W. Brooke

_____ 2. Sidney Poitier

_____ 3. Arthur Gaston

_____ 4. Charles Drew

_____ 5. Marian Anderson

_____ 6. Booker T. Washington

_____ 7. George Washington Carver

_____ 8. Frederick E. Davison

_____ 9. Frederick Douglass

_____ 10. Willie Mays

a. great baseball player

b. brilliant research surgeon

c. Brigadier General

d. great contralto singer

e. actor

f. outstanding abolitionist

g. millionaire businessman

h. founder of Tuskegee Institute

i. world-famous teacher and scientist

j. U. S. Senator

Evaluative Criteria: The students will successfully complete the worksheet on famous Black Americans.

Answer Key: 1j, 2e, 3g, 4b, 5d, 6h, 7i, 8c, 9f, 10a.

LESSON 14

Title: Come to the Festival!

Overview: This lesson is a culminating activity for a Social Studies unit of the medieval and early renaissance periods. The purpose is to involve students in activities related to the period of study by holding a festival where students and teachers dress in costumes, play games, prepare and eat food, dance, sing, and view or perform in skits and puppet shows.

Library Media Skills Objectives:

Identify and locate specific resources.

Interpret information found in resources.

Compare visual images from more than one source.

Compose a story based on information from resources.

Performance Objectives: Given a list of group activities for the festival, the students will work with their group to research, plan, and prepare an activity for the festival.

Subject Area: Social Studies, Language Arts, Reading Team.

Learning Strategy: Lecture, practice, role-playing, games, project.

Resources:

Books: Haley, Gail. *Costumes for Plays & Playing.*
Harris, Christie. *Figleafing through History.*
Schnurnberger, Lynn. *Kings, Queens, Knights & Jesters.*
Grunfeld, Frederick. *Games of the World.*
Cochrane, Louise. *Tabletop Theatres & Plays.*
Tichenor, Tom. *Folk Plays for Puppets You Can Make.*
Goodenough, S. *The Renaissance.*
Brown, Ivor. *Shakespeare and His World.*
Hartman, Gertrude. *Medieval Days and Ways.*

Transparencies: *Milliken: Medieval Period: Book One & Book Two.*

Records: Nonesuch. *Monteverdi/Madrigals.*

Food and drink.

Costumes.

Guidelines for Producing a Puppet Show.

Methods:

The teacher will:

1. Plan activities with team members and the library media specialist.
2. Determine schedule.
3. Assign a teacher to work with each group.
4. Participate in festival activities.
5. Evaluate activities.

The library media specialist will:

1. Identify print and nonprint resources.
2. Discuss resources and schedule with team leader.
3. Work with one activity group to plan, produce, and present a puppet show.
4. Participate in festival activities.

Activities:

1. In a large group meeting, the team leader will introduce the unit, define the objectives and procedures, discuss the evaluative criteria, present the schedule, divide the students into groups.

2. The students will work in the following groups: games, models, treasure hunt, skit, human chess game, puppet show, heralds.

3. Each group, under the direction of a teacher, will plan, research, and present an activity at the festival.

4. Each student will research, construct, and wear a period costume at the festival.

5. All students and team members will participate in the festival activities such as:
   • Parade.
   • Costume judging.
   • Human chess game.
   • Face painting.
   • Student-planned games.
   • Exhibits: models, charts, heralds.
   • Skits.
   • Treasure hunt.
   • Eat and drink, merrily.

Evaluative Criteria: The students will follow directions and successfully complete the assignments. At the end of the festival, they will evaluate each activity. The teacher working with each group will evaluate the accomplishments of each student in the group.

LESSON 15

Title: Let's Make a Crossword Puzzle.

Overview: The purpose of this lesson is for students to make a crossword puzzle based on facts about the contributions and life of a black musician. They will exchange puzzles and solve at least one puzzle.

Library Media Skills Objectives:

Locate reference material related to specific subject areas.

Select suitable print and nonprint material for a specified topic.

Use an index.

Make a bibliography.

Use *Readers' Guide to Periodical Literature.*

Performance Objective: Given a list of black musicians and a sample crossword puzzle to solve, the students will locate and list facts about the musician and make a bibliography. They will use these facts to make a crossword puzzle with clues. They will exchange puzzles and solve at least one puzzle.

Subject Area: Music.

Learning Strategy: Lecture, puzzle.

Resources:

Books: *Ebony Pictorial History of Black America.*
Current Biography.
New Century Cyclopedia of Names.
Ewen, David. *American Musical Theatre.*
Collier, James. *The Great Jazz Artists.*
Claghorn, Charles. *Biographical Dictionary of American Music.*
Readers' Guide to Periodical Literature.

Study Prints: *Famous Black Americans.* Audiovisual Enterprises.

Filmstrips: *Black Folk Music in America.* SVE.

Microcomputer Software, Apple II: *Crossword Magic.* L & S Computerware, Sunnyvale, Calif. (optional)

Sample Crossword Puzzle (see page 154).

BLACK MUSICIANS

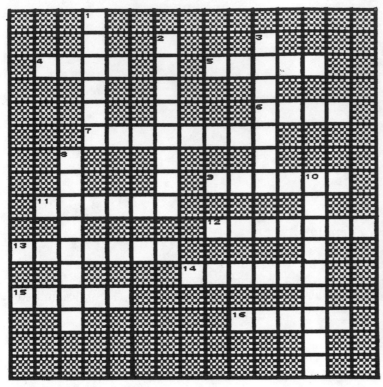

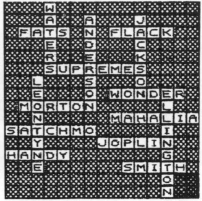

Answers: Black Musicians

ACROSS CLUES

4. ----Waller, jazz pianist and composer
5. Roberta -----, acclaimed at Newport Jazz Festival in 1972
6. Nat ---- Cole, singer who gave a command performance for Queen Elizabeth
7. The --------, trio who won seven gold records
9. Stevie ------, singer and pianist blind from birth
11. Jelly Roll ------, composer of "The Original Jelly Roll Blues"
12. ------- Jackson, outstanding gospel singer
13. Nickname of Louis Armstrong
14. Scott ------, king of ragtime
15. W.C. -----, composer of the "St. Louis Blues"
16. Bessie -----, one of the greatest women blues singers

DOWN CLUES

1. Ethel ------, celebrated gospel singer
2. Marian --------, first Black person to sing with the Metropolitan Opera
3. The ------- Five, brothers who formed a successful vocal group
8. -------- Price, a great soprano opera star
10. Duke ---------, band leader, pianist, and composer

Methods:

The teacher will:

1. Discuss performance objective and evaluative criteria.
2. Present suggestions of names of black musicians for research: Charlie Pride, Scott Joplin, Aretha Franklin, Mahalia Jackson, Andre Watts, Louis Armstrong, Bessie Smith, Stevie Wonder, W. C. Handy, Ethel Waters, Eubie Blake.
3. Assign a partner.
4. Schedule classes in the library media center.
5. Evaluate crossword puzzles.

The library media specialist will:

1. Present a lecture on special reference books in the field of music and biography.
2. Review the use of *Readers' Guide to Periodical Literature.*
3. Make a sample crossword puzzle.
4. Assist students in constructing a crossword puzzle.
5. Check finished crossword puzzles and clues using the bibliography.

The student will:

1. Work with a partner to solve the sample crossword puzzle.
2. Select the name of a black musician.
3. Locate facts about the musician using reference books, encyclopedias, and magazines.
4. List facts about the life of the black musician and the contributions made to music.
5. Make a bibliography of the sources used.
6. Construct a crossword puzzle that includes the name of the black musician.
7. Make clues that can be answered with facts from reference materials located in the library media center.
8. Turn in the completed assignment to the library media specialist:
   - List of facts and bibliography.
   - Crossword puzzle with clues.
   - Solution to crossword puzzle.
9. Solve at least one crossword puzzle made by other students.

Evaluative Criteria: The students will successfully make a crossword puzzle about a black musician. They will exchange puzzles and solve at least one crossword puzzle.

LESSON 16

Title: Marvelous Myths.

Overview: The purpose of this unit is to promote reading and encourage creativity through a study of mythology. The students will complete activities at four centers and will prepare a culminating project.

Library Media Skills Objectives:

Recognize different types of myths.

Identify characteristics of myths.

Select appropriate medium for presentation.

Performance Objective: Given background information about the basic human experiences embodied in mythology and given learning centers depicting myths of creation, seasons, heroes, and adventures, the students will complete the activities at each station and prepare a mythology project.

Subject Area: Reading.

Learning Strategy: Audiovisual instruction, practice, project.

Resources:

Books: Barber, Richard. *A Companion to World Mythology*.

Shapiro, Max, ed. *Mythologies of the World: A Concise Encyclopedia*.

Enslin, Bernard. *Heraclea: A Legend of Warrior Women*.

Eliot, Alexander. *Myths*.

Graves, Robert. *The Greek Myths*.

Hamilton, Edith. *Mythology*.

Cassette tapes: *Heroes, Gods, and Monsters*. Spoken Arts.

Filmstrips: *Myths of Greece and Rome*. SVE.

Mythology Lives! Ancient Stories and Modern Literature. The Center for Humanities, Inc.

Methods:

The teacher will:

1. Introduce the unit and explain the objectives.
2. Show the filmstrip series *Mythology Lives! Ancient Stories and Modern Literature* by The Center for Humanities, Inc.
3. Use the teacher's guide for ideas for discussion and review.

Methods (cont'd.)

4. Ask the library media specialist to provide resource materials for the learning centers and to assist students with projects.

5. Set up four learning centers: Myths of Creation, Myths of Seasons, Myths of Heroes, and Myths of Adventure.

6. Use the filmstrip for each station from the filmstrip series *Myths of Greece and Rome* by SVE.

7. Include appropriate books and topics at each station.

8. Ask the students to view the filmstrip and choose at least one tape and one story for study at each station.

9. Remind the students to take notes identifying the theme, common elements, characters, and plots.

10. Review the unit after the students have completed the stations.

11. Guide the students in choosing a culminating project by suggesting that they
    • Write a modern day myth.
    • Make a diorama.
    • Make a series of posters.
    • Record a radio broadcast of a myth.
    • Make a mythology web.
    • Use write-on slides to illustrate a Greek myth.
    • Take photographs of students posing as gods and heroes.
    • Create a book of mythological creatures.
    • Video tape a myth.

12. Evaluate the unit and projects.

The library media specialist will:

1. Preview and select resource materials on mythology.

2. Reserve and deliver print and nonprint materials to the classroom of the reading teacher.

3. Assist students with photography, video taping, radio broadcast, or hand drawn slide projects.

4. Invite students to use library media center facilities for projects.

5. Evaluate unit with the reading teacher. Discuss the effectiveness of the print and nonprint resources.

The students will:

1. View and discuss the filmstrip series *Mythology Lives! Ancient Stories and Modern Literature.*

2. Take notes at the four learning centers while viewing filmstrips and reading and listening to various myths.

3. Select a project from suggestions given by the teacher or decide on an original idea.

4. Work with a group or as an individual.

Methods (cont'd.)

5. Go to the library media center to complete research for project.
6. Ask the library media specialist for assistance with media related project.
7. Complete project and present to class.

Evaluative Criteria: The students will successfully complete the four learning centers and will complete a mythology project.

LESSON 17

Title: Book Quest.

Overview: The purpose of this unit is to promote reading of the Newbery Award books. Using *Super Seven*, an activities booklet by Virginia Mealy that is published by Book Lures, Inc., students will choose from a list of seven books and complete the activities on one Newbery Medal winner.

Library Media Skills Objectives:

Identify and describe the Newbery Medal Award.

Identify authors and their work.

Performance Objective: Given information about the Newbery Medal Award and seven Newbery Award winning books and their authors, the students will read at least one of the books and complete the activities at a learning center.

Subject Area: Reading.

Learning Strategy: Discussion, reading, learning center.

Resources:

Books: Mealy, Virginia. *Super Seven.**

Newbery Medal Books: Daugherty, James. *Daniel Boone.*

Sperry, Armstrong. *Call It Courage.*

Henry, Marguerite. *King of the Wind.*

deAngeli, Marguerite. *The Door in the Wall.*

Wojciechowska, Maia. *Shadow of a Bull.*

Konigsburg, Elaine. *From the Mixed-Up Files of Mrs. Basil E. Frankweiler.*

O'Brien, Robert. *Mrs. Frisby and the Rats of NIMH.*

Miller, Bertha. *Newbery Medal Books: 1922-1955.*

Kergmar, Lee. *Newbery and Caldecott Medal Books: 1956-1965.*

Kergmar, Lee. *Newbery and Caldecott Medal Books: 1966-1975.*

Bookmarks of Newbery Medal Books.

Methods:

The teacher will:

1.   Plan the unit with the library media specialist who will have the primary responsibility of this unit.

2.   Schedule the class in the library media center for the introduction and selection of the books and two weeks later for the learning center activities.

---

*The *Super Seven* activities booklet is available from Book Lures, Inc., Box 9450, O'Fallon, MO 63366.

Methods (cont'd.)

The library media specialist will:

1. Purchase at least five paperback copies of the Newbery Award books listed in the resource section.

2. Use the book *Super Seven* by Virginia Mealy for information on the Newbery Award, authors, and activities with seven Newbery Award books.

3. Read all seven of the books and prepare a book and author talk.

4. Set up learning centers for each book using two or three activities from *Super Seven*.

5. Purchase or make bookmarks that contain the authors and titles of Newbery Medal winners since 1922.

6. Grade activity sheets.

7. Evaluate the unit with the teacher.

The students will:

1. Discuss the Newbery Medal Award.

2. Choose a book to read from the seven titles presented by the library media specialist.

3. Complete the activities at the learning center after reading the book.

4. Receive a bookmark with the names of all Newbery Medal Awards.

Evaluative Criteria: The students will read a book from the titles presented by the library media specialist and will successfully complete the activities at the learning center.

LESSON 18

Title: Let's Play Games.

Overview: The purpose of this lesson is to illustrate the approach to media instruction through the use of games developed by Jeanne Wieckert and Irene Bell in *Media/Classroom Skills: Games for Middle School,* Vols. 1 & 2.

Library Media Skills Objectives:

Use a dictionary to find derivation.

Use a glossary.

Skim materials to find a word.

Find specific information using key words and phrases.

Performance Objectives:

1. Given the game "Incorporation" from *Media/Classroom Skills: Games for Middle School,* Vol. 1, the students will use resources in the library media center to find French words that have been incorporated into the English language.

2. Given the game "Shoot and Score" from *Media/Classroom Skills: Games for Middle School,* Vol. 2 and reference books on basketball, the students will locate and give appropriate answers in two minutes to questions concerning the game and follow directions for completing the game.

Subject Area: French, Physical Education.

Learning Strategy: Games.

Resources:

1. Game: "Incorporation"
   Books: French dictionaries, French textbooks, language books.

2. Game: "Shoot and Score," gameboard, 30 index cards bearing questions of the game, 1 spinner, 10 triangle cards.
   Book: Hickok, Ralph. *New Encyclopedia of Sports.*

Methods: For game "Incorporation."

The French teacher will:
1. Give examples of French words assimilated into the English language.
2. Divide students into two teams.
3. Give procedures for playing game.
4. Send students to library media center.
5. Check answer sheets from each team.

Methods for "Incorporation" (cont'd.)

The library media specialist will:

1. Compile a list of French words assimilated into the English language before students are given the game to assure that answers are available to students.

2. Observe students as they search for answers.

3. Encourage students to search for answers but do not give assistance.

The students will:

1. Use dictionaries and other sources to compile a list of French words incorporated into English.

2. Give answer sheet to teacher.

3. Review lists by both teams after winner is announced.

Methods: For game "Shoot and Score."

The physical education teacher will:

1. Write 30 questions on colored index cards concerning the game of basketball.

2. Prepare the gameboard; obtain all materials.

3. Write 10 triangle card directions.

4. Send four students who are not able to take physical education that day with a note to the library media center to play the game "Shoot and Score."

The library media specialist will:

1. Reserve a place for the game "Shoot and Score" for use when needed by students.

2. Collect reference books on basketball rules to be used with game.

3. Serve as referee, if necessary.

4. Declare the winner.

The students will:

1. Read directions for playing the game "Shoot and Score."

2. Answer questions concerning basketball, if they know the answers. If not, locate each answer within two minutes by using the index or glossary of books on reserve with game. If incorrect answers are given, the guard will pass the play to the next player.

3. Continue play until winner is declared.

Evaluative Criteria: The students will use resources in the library media center to play the games "Incorporation" and "Shoot and Score."

LESSON 19

Title: Books to Cry By.

Overview: The purpose of this lesson is to promote reading of realistic fiction that provokes deep emotional feelings and response by the reader.

Library Media Skills Objectives:

Choose reading as a leisure-time activity.

Make a bibliography.

Performance Objective: Given a book talk, the students will select a book to read for pleasure.

Subject Area: Reading.

Learning Strategy: Book talk, discussion.

Resources:

Byars, Betsy. *Summer of the Swans.*

Cleaver, Vera, and Bill Cleaver. *Where the Lilies Bloom.*

Craven, Margaret. *I Heard the Owl Call My Name.*

Lowry, Lois. *A Summer to Die.*

Rodowsky, Colby. *What about Me?*

Smith, Doris. *A Taste of Blackberries.*

Methods:

The teacher will:
1. Discuss the lesson with the library media specialist.
2. Schedule the class in the library media center.
3. Allow students free reading time in class.
4. Ask students to keep a list of books read for pleasure in their reading notebook. List should contain author, title, place of publication, publisher, and copyright date.
5. Not require a book report or project.

The library media specialist will:
1. Keep a card file of books read.
    Make annotations.
    List passages for reading aloud.
2. Start pulling books for book report several weeks before class is scheduled to ensure the availability of desired titles.
3. Display books for book talk on large rack that allows book covers to be seen by students.

Methods (cont'd.)

4. Arrange books in sequence for use during book talk.
   Mark passages for reading aloud.

5. Have two boxes of facial tissues on table.
   Use one and pass one to class.

6. Introduce the book talk by asking students to name some events that happen to people that make them sad (death of a loved one, illness of someone close to you, failing a test, quarreling with a best friend, someone you like is moving away, having something destroyed by fire or flood, being in an accident, being alone, losing a contest, death of a pet, someone you love is getting a divorce, losing something you value, losing a basketball or football game, being broke, saying goodbye.)

7. State that many authors write realistic fiction depicting many of the events we have discussed. They use realistic events, problems, or conflicts that have happened or that could happen to build a fictitious plot for a story. The stories can be so convincing that they involve the reader in the situation, stir the heart, and evoke responses of grief and sadness.

8. Tell the students that they will hear about books today that may make them cry.

9. Give book talk "Books to Cry By" (see resource list). Vary the presentation by telling about certain books and reading very sad sections of other books. Don't hesitate to shed a few tears as you read or tell about the books. Let your emotions show. Use your facial tissues and pass around a box to students.

10. Make your book talks brief enough to entice the students to want to read the book.

The students will:

1. Go to the library media center for a book talk.

2. Discuss events that happen to people that make them sad.

3. Use active listening skills during the book talk.

4. Select a book to read.

5. Prepare a bibliography listing books read.

Evaluative Criteria: The students will participate in a book talk and will select a book to read.

LESSON 20

Title: The Past Is Prologue.

Overview: The purpose of this lesson is to stimulate students to read a historical fiction book of their choice for their enjoyment.

Library Media Skills Objectives:

Recognize different types of realistic fiction.

Select reading as a leisure-time activity.

Use card catalog.

Performance Objective: Given the characteristics of historical fiction and a review of the use of the card catalog, the students will use the card catalog to locate a historical fiction book.

Subject Area: Reading.

Learning Strategy: Discussion, book talk, practice, learning center.

Resources:

Examples of catalog cards.

Books for book talks: Beckman, Thea. *Crusade in Jeans.*
                         Paterson, Katherine. *Sign of the Chrysanthemum.*
                         Sutcliff, Rosemary. *Blood Feud.*

Filmstrips: Guidance Associates. *Reading for the Fun of It: Historical Fiction.*
               The Bronze Bow. Miller-Brody.
               The Door in the Wall. Miller-Brody.
               The High King. Miller-Brody.
               Johnny Tremain. Miller-Brody.

Information card (see page 166).

Methods:

The teacher will:
1.   Discuss the characteristics of historical fiction.
2.   Explain the objectives of reading for enjoyment.
3.   Schedule one class period for book talks and one for learning center activities.

The library media specialist will:
1.   Dress in costumes to present book talks on historical fiction.
2.   Use transparencies to show examples of catalog card subject headings of historical fiction books.
3.   Utilize filmstrips for learning centers.

Methods (cont'd.)

The students will:

1. Listen to book talks.
2. View filmstrips in learning centers.
3. Locate titles and authors of historical fiction in the card catalog.
4. Select and read a historical fiction book of their choice for their enjoyment.
5. Complete the following information card for the teacher:

Sample Information Card

Name _____

Date _____

I have read the following historical fiction book:

Author _____

Title _____

Publisher _____

Copyright date _____

Place and historical period _____

_____

Evaluative Criteria: The students will locate, select, and read a historical fiction book of their choice for their enjoyment. They will not be required to make a report or project.

LESSON 21

Title: "R. G. T. P. L.–Over!"

Overview: The purpose of this lesson is to teach students to use the *Readers' Guide to Periodical Literature* in order to locate information in magazines on catastrophes that have happened during the past five years. The students will complete a chart on worldwide catastrophes.

Library Media Skills Objective:

Use *Readers' Guide to Periodical Literature.*

Performance Objective: Given instruction in the use of the *Readers' Guide to Periodical Literature* and background information on catastrophes, the students will locate information in magazines to complete a chart on worldwide catastrophes from 1978-1983.

Subject Area: Social Studies.

Learning Strategy: Discussion, demonstration, practice.

Resources:

Record: *Edward R. Murrow "I Can Hear It Now" 1933-1945.* Columbia Records.

Dictionaries.

Readers' Guide to Periodical Literature.

Magazines.

Worldwide Catastrophes Chart (see page 168).

Magazine request slips (see page 168).

Transparencies for teaching use of *Readers' Guide to Periodical Literature* (see page 169).

Methods:

The teacher will:

1. Plan the unit with the library media specialist and decide on areas of responsibility for teaching.
2. Introduce the unit by playing excerpts from the record *Edward R. Murrow "I Can Hear It Now" 1933-1945.*
3. Ask the students to define:

catastrophes	drought
disasters	assassination
hurricane	volcano eruption
tornado	explosion
flood	plague
typhoon	famine
monsoon	shipwreck
earthquake	fire
tidal wave	atomic power plant—
avalanche	accidents and explosions

Give out dictionaries and ask students to find the best meanings.

(Text continues on page 170.)

Sample Worldwide Catastrophes Chart

Name of Catastrophe	Cause (Man or Nature)	Country	Year	Description of Event

---

Sample Magazine Request Slips

Your Name:_____ Table Number:_____

Title of magazine:_____

Date of magazine:_____

Title of article: _____

Pages of article: _____

TRANSPARENCIES

READERS' GUIDE TO
PERIODICAL LITERATURE

An author/subject INDEX to
periodicals of general
interest published in the
United States

ABBREVIATIONS OF
PERIODICALS INDEXED

Use list in copies of Readers'
Guide to Periodical
Literature

PERIODICALS INDEXED

Use list in copies of Readers'
Guide to Periodical Literature

ABBREVIATIONS

Use list in copies of
Readers' Guide to Periodical Literature

CUMULATIVE

Published semimonthly
Quarterly cumulative issue
Yearly cumulative bound issue

SUBJECT ENTRY

AUTHOR ENTRY

SEE REFERENCE

SEE ALSO REFERENCE

Sample Entry:

FLOODS— Subject entry
By Land and By Sea— Title of article
il Newsweek— Title of magazine
82:39— Volume and page
S 10 '73- Date of magazine

Methods (cont'd.)

    4.   Discuss historical catastrophes

> San Francisco earthquake
> Titanic
> Dirigible Hindenburg
> Chicago fire
> 1972 Olympics

    5.   Give out chart on worldwide catastrophes. Tell the students that they will complete the charts by using magazines from 1978 to 1983. The library media specialist will instruct them in using an index to locate their magazines, the *Readers' Guide to Periodical Literature.*

    6.   Schedule classes in the library media center for instruction and research.

    7.   Divide students into five groups.

    8.   Check and grade completed charts.

    9.   Evaluate unit with library media specialist.

The library media specialist will:

1.   Prepare transparencies for teaching the use of *Readers' Guide to Periodical Literature.*

2.   On each table arrange cumulative copies (semimonthly, quarterly, and yearly) of *Readers' Guide to Periodical Literature* for the years 1978-1983.

3.   Use transparencies and copies of *Readers' Guide to Periodical Literature* for discussion with class involvement, flashing the transparencies on the screen to focus student attention during the discussion.

4.   Give the students magazine request slips. Tell them to locate entries in the *Readers' Guide to Periodical Literature* on catastrophes and complete the request slips.

5.   Collect request slips and ask student aides to locate magazines for next class period.

6.   Set up table with magazines requested and copies of *Readers' Guide to Periodical Literature* for the second session of the unit.

7.   Deliver additional magazines as requested.

8.   Evaluate unit by observing students' use of *Readers' Guide to Periodical Literature.*

The students will:

1.   Listen to record.

2.   Use dictionaries to define terms.

3.   Discuss historical catastrophes.

4.   Follow directions given by the library media specialist in using the *Readers' Guide to Periodical Literature.*

5.   Use information in magazines to complete the "Worldwide Catastrophes Chart."

Evaluative Criteria: The students will correctly use the *Readers' Guide to Periodical Literature* to locate information in magazines to complete the "Worldwide Catastrophes Chart."

LESSON 22

Title: More Basics.

Overview: The purpose of this unit is to extend the students' knowledge of the history and development of computers, computer-related terminology, and the capabilities and limitations of computers.

Library Media Skills Objectives:

Identify computer hardware and software.

Utilize computer hardware and software.

Performance Objective: Given background information on the history and development of computers and a computer resource center, the students will keep a computer literacy notebook listing facts about the history and development of computers, computer-related terminology, and the capabilities and limitations of computers.

Subject Area: Math.

Learning Strategy: Audiovisual instruction, discussion, project.

Resources:

Microcomputer Software with filmstrip: *Introduction to Computers.* SVE.

Manuals for computers.

Filmstrips: *Computers: From Pebbles to Programs.* Guidance Associates.

Books: Evans, Christopher. *The Making of the Micro: A History of the Computer.*
Frederick, Franz. *Guide to Microcomputers.*
Ahl, David, cd. *The Best of Creative Computing,* Vols. 1, 2, and 3.
Ahl, David, ed. *Computers in Mathematics: A Sourcebook of Ideas.*
Billings, Karen, and David Moursund. *Are You Computer Literate?*
Deken, Joseph. *The Electronic Cottage.*
Evans, Christopher. *The Micro Millennium.*
D'Ignazio, Fred. *Small Computers: Exploring Their Technology and Future.*
Willis, Jerry, and Merl Miller. *Computers for Everybody.*
Drefus, Herbert. *What Computers Can't Do: The Limits of Artificial Intelligence.*
Haugo, John. *Computer Literacy: Introduction to Microcomputers.*
Schneideman, Marty. *Glossary of Computer Terms.*

Magazines: *Creative Computing.*
Classroom Computer News.
Softside.

Resources (cont'd.)

Magazine Articles: Sherouse, Vicki. "Support Your Local Computer Revolution." *The Book Report* (September/October 1982): 40-42.

Anderson, Eric. "One More Piece of AV Equipment." *The Book Report* (September/October 1982): 28-32.

"Glossary." *Commodore: The Microcomputer Magazine* (April/May 1983): 36-39.

Methods:

The teacher will:

1. Plan the unit with the library media specialist.

2. Ask the library media specialist to set up a computer resource center in the library media center.

3. Introduce the unit and explain the objectives to the students.

4. Show the filmstrip *Computers: From Pebbles to Programs* and lead a discussion on the history and development of computers.

5. Ask students to take notes and list pertinent facts in a computer literacy notebook.

6. Have students divide their notebooks into four parts: (1) history and development of computers, (2) computer-related terminology, (3) capabilities of computers, and (4) limitations of computers.

7. Let small groups of students use the computer resource center in the library media center when they have completed math assignments.

8. Tell students to use books, magazines, newspapers, and manuals to begin compiling facts for their computer literacy notebook.

9. Collect and grade the notebooks in one month.

10. Analyze data and discuss with class.

The library media specialist will:

1. Set up a computer resource center adjacent to the computer center in the library media center.

   Order materials for the center.

2. Ask teachers and students to add magazine and newspaper articles to the center.

3. Assist groups of students in using the center.

The students will:

1. View and discuss the filmstrip *Computers: From Pebbles to Programs.*

2. Set up a computer literacy notebook.

3. Compile data on the history and development of computers, computer-related terminology, capabilities of computers, and limitations of computers.

4. Use the computer resource center in the library media center.

5. Use the public library, college libraries, and talk with people who work with computers (an optional activity).

6. Turn in notebook.

7. Discuss data with class.

Evaluative Criteria: The students will complete a computer literacy notebook giving data on the history and development of computers, computer-related terminology, capabilities of computers, and limitations of computers.

LESSON 23

Title: Big Time Productions.

Overview: The impact of advertising is keenly felt by middle school students. As they view television, listen to the radio, read magazines and newspapers, and spend hours in shopping malls, they are bombarded with advertisements. To help them identify propaganda, fact, and opinion, the students will complete assignments concerning advertising techniques and use these techniques to create their own commercials on video tape.

Library Media Skills Objectives:

Locate and utilize all necessary sources to gather information for a specified subject.

Distinguish between fact and opinion.

Utilize organizational skills to produce a video tape recording.

Performance Objectives:

1. Given magazines, newspaper advertisements, and other printed materials, the students will be able to identify propaganda, fact, opinion, and other techniques used in writing advertisements.

2. Using examples from magazines and newspapers, students will make propaganda/advertisement booklets to illustrate the use of different types of advertising techniques.

3. After viewing and analyzing commercials on television, the students will create their own commercials on video tape employing these techniques. They will work in assigned groups to write a script, make a storyboard, prepare graphics and scenery, rehearse scenes, and produce a commercial on video tape.

Subject Area: Reading.

Learning Strategy: Reading, practice, viewing, discussion, audiovisual project.

Resources:

Magazines and Newspapers.

Books: Mitchell, Malcolm G. *Propaganda, Polls, and Public Opinion: Are the People Manipulated?*

Article: *Propaganda.* Encyclopaedia Britannica.

Pamphlets: *How a Television Commercial Is Made.* Texaco.

Group Guidelines

Group Report Form

Storyboard Worksheet (see page 119).

Group Guidelines

Audiovisual Project: Plan and produce a commercial on video tape.

1. Brainstorm ideas.
2. Determine objective.
3. Select product.
4. Write script.
5. Assign duties.
   a. Write storyboard.
   b. Prepare graphics and scenery.
   c. Select actors.
6. Rehearse scenes.
7. Produce video tape.
8. Evaluate.

Group Report Form

Date:_____

Chairman:_____

Group members:_____

Group report:_____

_____

Goal accomplished today:_____

_____

Goals for tomorrow:_____

_____

Methods:

The teacher will:

1. Lead a discussion on propaganda, fact, and opinion by giving examples of each.
2. Analyze techniques used in advertising.
3. Assign propaganda/advertisement booklets.
4. Schedule library media center activities with library media specialist.
5. Divide class into groups. Appoint chairmen.
6. Explain group guidelines.

The library media specialist will:

1. Conduct a discussion about the purposes of commercials and the impact on the consumer.
2. Present pamphlet "How a Television Commercial Is Made."
3. Show video demonstration of student-made commercials.
4. Assist students with planning and producing a commercial on video tape.
5. View and evaluate student productions.

The students will:

1. Identify propaganda, fact, and opinion used in advertisements.
2. Illustrate advertisement/propaganda techniques in booklet form.
3. View and analyze television commercials.
4. Work with an assigned group of students to plan, create, and produce a video taped commercial.

Evaluative Criteria: The students will correctly illustrate propaganda/advertisement techniques in booklet form. They will work with their assigned group to successfully plan and produce a commercial on videotape. Each group will be graded daily on accomplishments and work habits. The chairman is responsible for turning in a group report each day. These reports will be returned to the chairman with comments from the teacher and/or the library media specialist.

8

Skills Lessons for Grade Eight

Title: Discover the Discoverer.

Overview: The purpose of this unit is to encourage students to discover the fascinating facts about the discovery and exploration of the New World. They will locate information about an explorer, trace the route of their explorer on a map, and present an oral report to the class.

Library Media Skills Objectives:

Use atlases, almanacs, biographical dictionaries.

Use subject headings in card catalog.

Use Dewey Decimal System of Classification.

Use encyclopedias.

Performance Objective: Given the name of an explorer and a blank map, the students will locate information about the explorer, trace the route of their explorer on the blank map, and will prepare and present an oral report to the class.

Subject Area: Social Studies.

Learning Strategy: Audiovisual instruction, lecture, practice.

Resources:

Books: Keating, Bern. *Famous American Explorers.*

Bakeless, Katherine, and John Bakeless. *They Saw America First.*

Buehr, Walter. *The Spanish Conquistadors in North America.*

Kerby, Elizabeth. *The Conquistadors.*

Resources (cont'd.)

Berry, E., and H. Best. *Men Who Changed the Map.*

Buehr, Walter. *The Portuguese Explorers.*

Rich, Louise. *New World Explorers.*

Golding, Morton. *The Mystery of the Viking in America.*

Norman, C. *Discoverers of America.*

Clark, William. *Explorers of the World.*

National Geographic Index.

Magazine Articles: "Christopher Columbus." *National Geographic* (November 1975): 584-625.

"Sir Francis Drake." *National Geographic* (February 1975): 216-233.

"Reach for the New World." *National Geographic* (December 1977): 724-769.

Globe.

Filmstrips: *Age of Exploration.* Warren Schloat.

Age of Exploration and Discovery. Coronet.

Great Explorers. National Geographic.

List of Explorers:

Balboa	DeSoto
Cabot	DeVaca
Cabral	Drake
Cabrillo	Ericson
Cartier	Joliet
Champlain	LaSalle
Columbus	Magellan
Coronado	Marquette
Cortes	Pizarro
DeGama	Verrazano
DeLeon	

Methods:

The teacher will:

1. Introduce a unit by showing filmstrip series.

2. Review mapmaking skills.

3. Discuss the objectives and research topics with the library media specialist.

4. Schedule the classes in the library media center.

5. Provide outline maps for students.

Methods (cont'd.)

6. Make a list of explorers. Cut the list into strips. Let students pick a name from a small chest or bowl.

7. Accompany students to the library media center.

8. Evaluate oral reports.

The library media specialist will:

1. Give a brief review of reference and research skills:
   - Card catalog subject headings:
     EXPLORERS   AMERICA–DISCOVERY AND EXPLORATION
   - Dewey Decimal Classification:
     910.9   973.1   920   921
   - Indexes:
     National Geographic Index.
     World Book and *Compton's Encyclopedias.*
   - Biographical References:
     Webster's Biographical Dictionary.
     New Century Cyclopedia of Names.
   - Atlases:
     Newby, Eric. *World Atlas of Exploration.*
   - Bibliography notation:
     Author, title, place of publication, publisher, copyright date.
     Title of article, name of encyclopedia, volume number, copyright date, page number.

2. Assist students with research questions.

3. Evaluate unit with teacher.

The students will:

1. Pick a name of an explorer.

2. Take notes on lecture given by library media specialist.

3. Use research skills to locate information on explorer.

4. Trace the route of their explorer on the blank map. Label the map and make a legend.

5. Prepare and present an oral report on an explorer including nationality, accomplishments, and several fascinating facts.

Evaluative Criteria: The students will prepare and present an oral report on an explorer and include a map showing the route of the explorer.

LESSON 2

Title: Le Français dans le Monde—Bon Voyage!

Overview: The purpose of this lesson is for the students to locate information and prepare a report on a country where the French language is spoken. The report will be presented orally in class.

Library Media Skills Objectives:

Use general reference works.

Use vertical file.

Compare figures in maps and graphs.

Use bibliographies as an aid in locating information.

Use appropriate A-V equipment for selected presentations.

Utilize organizational skills.

Use card catalog to locate nonprint material.

Performance Objective: Given the name of a country where the French language is spoken and a worksheet with instructions, the students will locate and utilize specific facts to prepare an oral report for presentation to the class.

Subject Area: French.

Learning Strategy: Lecture, practice, project.

Resources:

National Geographic Index.

Readers' Guide to Periodical Literature.

Vertical file.

World Almanac.

Maps.

Charts.

Records.

Filmstrips.

Telephone directory: Travel Agents.
Embassy.

Statesman's Yearbook.

People of the Earth.

Worldmark Encyclopedia.

Resources (cont'd.)

Atlas.

Public Library.

People who have lived in French-speaking countries.

Worksheet Instructions (see page 182).

Methods:

The teacher will:

1.   Make a list of countries where the French language is spoken.

2.   Let students select one country for their report.

3.   Explain the worksheet instructions.

The library media specialist will:

1.   Display a map of the world with the location of French-speaking nations.

2.   Play a French song to introduce the lesson.

3.   Review and demonstrate use of reference sources, e.g., *Readers' Guide to Periodical Literature, National Geographic Index, Statesman's Yearbook.*

4.   Prepare bibliography of resources.

5.   Remind students to visit public libraries and travel agents and to use interlibrary loan.

6.   Assist students in locating telephone numbers and addresses of embassies.

7.   Assist students with research and preparation of report.

8.   Guide students in use of audiovisual equipment, e.g., filmstrip projector, slide projector, opaque projector.

The students will:

1.   Gather information, take notes, write speech, make an outline and bibliography, prepare oral presentation.

2.   Make a map, poster, or flag.

3.   Show slides, filmstrip, film, pictures, or posters.

4.   Give oral presentation using several audiovisual aids.

Evaluative Criteria: The students will complete an outline and bibliography. They will give an oral presentation that meets the worksheet instructions.

Le Français dans le Monde—Bon Voyage!
Instructions

Step 1: Gather information.
   a. Go to the library media center and find as many resources as you can about your country. You must use at least three resources, including one periodical.
   b. Go to a public or college library.
   c. Contact an embassy.
   d. Visit a travel agency. (optional)

Step 2: Look for information about
   a. population.
   b. location.
   c. major cities.
   d. sites to visit.
   e. languages spoken.
   f. money (compare to U. S. dollars).
   g. climate.
   h. products.
   i. culture.
   j. foods.

Step 3: Record information.
   a. Take notes in your own words.
   b. Prepare a bibliography of resources used.
   c. Make an outline.

Step 4: Make a travel presentation.
   a. Give a five- to ten-minute speech on your country using at least one visual aid.
   b. Use your note cards and talk to the group.
   c. Prepare a travel poster with the name of your country and a slogan in French.
   d. For your presentation, you may use slides, pictures, filmstrips, film, or music. You may dress like the people of your specific country and serve a sample of food eaten in your country.
   e. Schedule:
   Week 1—Your notes will be checked.
   Week 2—Rough copy of outline will be checked.
   Week 3—Written outline and bibliography due. Oral presentations begin.

LESSON 3

Title: You Be the Judge.

Overview: The purpose of this unit is to assist gifted and talented students in preparing for a debate. They will utilize research and organizational skills, upper level critical thinking skills, and logical, concise presentation skills.

Library Media Skills Objectives:

Select proper sources for information on specified subjects.

Use vertical file to obtain materials such as pamphlets, pictures, or clippings.

Use *Readers' Guide to Periodical Literature.*

Use bibliographies as an aid in locating information.

Use specified reference materials to develop and support research.

Evaluate material for accuracy and/or appropriateness.

Identify unsubstantiated statements or facts.

Utilize organizational skills: outlining, note taking.

Distinguish between fact and opinion.

Recognize availability of suitable material in public libraries.

Performance Objective: Given a sample debate on video tape to critique and a list of debate topics, the students will select, research, organize, and debate a topic.

Subject Area: Language Arts (Gifted and Talented).

Learning Strategy: Demonstration, lecture, practice.

Resources:

Facts on File.

SIRS Social Issues Research Series: Death and Dying, Crime, Aging, Defense.

Encyclopedias.

Vertical file materials.

Readers' Guide to Periodical Literature.

Books: Gilford, Henry. *How to Give a Speech.*

Zerman, Melvyn. *Beyond a Reasonable Doubt: Inside the American Jury System.*

LeShan, Eda. *The Roots of Crime: What You Need to Know about Crime and What You Can Do about It.*

Encyclopedia of Sociology.

Resources (cont'd.)

Microfilm: Magazines.

Public libraries.

Video tape, filmstrip, or movie on debating.

Methods:

The teacher will:

1. Plan lesson with the library media specialist.
2. Present an overview of the principles and the terms and concepts of debating.
3. Show a video tape (or film or filmstrip) of a debate.
4. Lead a discussion on debating techniques focusing on divergent thinking skills and problem solving strategies.
5. Provide activities to assist students in distinguishing between fact or opinion, identifying and reporting unsubstantiated statements or facts.
6. Ask library media specialist to come to the class to review research skills:
   - use of *Readers' Guide to Periodical Literature.*
   - use of bibliographies.
   - use of vertical file.
   - use of special reference sources: *SIRS.*
7. Prepare a list of debate topics:

Euthanasia	Conscription for Women
Gun Control	Child Abuse
Censorship	Nuclear Weapons
Welfare	

8. Let students decide debate topics and form debate teams.
9. Schedule classes in the library media center.
10. Schedule video taping sessions.
11. Obtain judges for debate.
12. Evaluate unit with the library media specialist.

The library media specialist will:

1. Meet with the teacher to jointly plan the unit.
2. Obtain resources.
3. Review research skills with students.
4. Remind students about the availability of materials in the public library.
5. Assist students with location, research, and organization of resources.
6. Videotape debate.
7. Evaluate unit.

Methods (cont'd.)

The students will:

1. Learn the techniques of debating.
2. Choose topic.
3. Locate and utilize resources.
4. Organize notes.
5. Participate in a debate.
6. View and evaluate video tape of debate.

Evaluative Criteria: The students will select a topic for a debate, locate and utilize resources, organize information, and will debate a topic.

LESSON 4

Title: Careers: A Look Ahead.

Overview: The purpose of this lesson is to provide research opportunities on careers for students as a part of a careers unit. After completing lessons using decision-making processes to explore interests and aptitudes and relating them to career preferences, students will select at least two careers to investigate. They will complete a job brief on each occupation.

Library Media Skills Objectives:

Use all necessary sources that are available to gather information for a specified subject.

Select suitable print and nonprint material for a specified topic.

Paraphrase or summarize material.

Find specific information using visuals and listening to audio materials.

Performace Objective: Given a Job Brief Form, learning centers with print and nonprint material on careers, and guidelines for interviews, the student will complete at least two job briefs. They will participate in a simulated video taped interview for one of their chosen occupations.

Subject Area: Social Studies.

Learning Strategy: Audiovisual instruction, learning center.

Resources:

Filmstrips: *Exploring Careers.* SVE.

  Livelyhoods—Careers for Your Life Style. Houghton Mifflin.

Microfiche: *COIN.* Bell and Howell.

Charts: *COPS Occupational Cluster Charts.*

Films: *Decisions, Decisions.* Churchill.

Pamphlets: *COPS.* Career Information Brief. Edits.

Books: *Encyclopedia of Careers and Vocational Guidance.*

  Dictionary of Occupational Titles.

  Occupational Outlook Handbook.

  Norback, Craig T., ed. *Careers Encyclopedia.*

  Alexander, Sue. *Finding Your First Job.*

  Brent, Patricia. *Crafts Careers.*

  Doyle, Robert. *Careers in Elective Government*

  Dunbar, Robert. *Zoology Careers.*

  Harmon, Margaret. *Working with Words: Careers for Writers.*

  Horton, Louise. *Careers in Office Work.*

Resources (cont'd.)

Job Brief Form (see page 188).

Interview Form (see page 189).

Guidance Counselor.

Career Stations

Folders for each station contain clippings and pamphlets from the vertical file, reprints from *Occupational Outlook Handbook.*

Stations reflect the 16 career interest categories:

1. Health Careers
2. Consumer & Homemaking
3. Transportation
4. Personal Services
5. Marine Science
6. Environment
7. Construction
8. Communication & Media
9. Fine Arts & Humanities
10. Manufacturing
11. Public Services
12. Agri-Business
13. Business & Office
14. Marketing & Distribution
15. Recreation & Hospitality
16. Science & Technology

Methods:

The teacher will:

1. Plan the lesson with the library media specialist. The guidance counselor will serve as a resource person.
2. Introduce the Job Brief Form and show an example of a completed form.
3. Explain the procedures for the video taped interview.
4. Schedule classes in the media center.
5. Accompany the class to the media center and assist students in locating and interpreting career information.
6. Grade job briefs.
7. View and evaluate video taped job interviews with the class, the library media specialist, and the guidance counselor.

The library media specialist will:

1. Reserve books and nonprint materials.
2. Compile career folders for the 16 career interest categories including clippings and pamphlets.
3. Make large signs with numbers 1-16. Set up 16 learning centers. Include career folder, print and nonprint materials, and equipment needed for each center.
4. Make a ditto directory map showing the location and title of the 16 interest categories.
5. Obtain films from county film library and set up viewing area for films and microfiche.
6. Demonstrate use of microfiche projector and other equipment as needed.
7. Help students use reference books and nonprint materials to locate specific information.
8. Videotape simulated interviews with students applying for jobs.

Job Brief Form

Title of job _____

Describe the job in a brief statement (typical daily duties) _____

_____

_____

_____

Working conditions _____

_____

Education and training required _____

_____

Skills and aptitudes _____

_____

Pay _____

Job opportunities _____

_____

Advantages _____

_____

Disadvantages _____

_____

Sources of information _____

_____

_____

Interview Form

Inteviewer will ask the following questions:

1. What job are you applying for?

2. What do you think your duties would be?

3. What are your qualifications?

4. Why are you interested in this job?

5. What salary would you expect?

Methods (cont'd.)

9. Evaluate unit with teacher and guidance counselor.
10. Assess need for additional materials.

The students will:

1. View movies and filmstrips, listen to tapes, and read about a number of careers.
2. Explore occupations through the concept of clusters.
3. Select two occupations from an interest inventory.
4. Locate learning center for the two occupations selected. Find information by using resources in center. Complete job brief.
5. Use microfiche to locate additional information on occupations.
6. Work with another student to write script for a simulated interview. Rehearse scenes.
7. Videotape simulated interview.
8. View interviews with entire class.
9. Discuss strengths and weaknesses of interviews.

Evaluative Criteria: The students will successfully complete at least two job briefs and a simulated video taped interview.

LESSON 5

Title: Let's Get Poetic!

Overview: The purpose of this unit is to give students in-depth learning experiences with poetry. They will review a variety of poetic forms, read many poems, use a poetry index, and complete a creative activity.

Library Media Skills Objectives:

Recognize a variety of poetic forms.

Use an index to locate material.

Select reading material relevant to interests and purposes.

Prepare a media presentation that expresses a mood or feeling.

Produce audiovisual project.

Performance Objective: Given a review of poetic forms and poetry indexes and given a list of activities, the students will select and read at least ten poems and will complete one activity.

Subject Area: Language Arts.

Learning Strategy: Audiovisual instruction, demonstration, practice, project.

Resources:

Sound Filmstrip: *Understanding Poetry.* SVE.

A Pocketful of Poetry. Guidance Associates.

Books: Hopkins, Lee. *To Look at Any Thing.*

Koch, Kenneth, et. al. *Wishes, Lies, & Dreams: Teaching Children to Write Poetry.*

Lewis, Claudia. *Poems of Earth and Space.*

Lueders, Edward and Primus St. John, eds. *Zero Makes Me Hungry: A Collection of Poems for Today.*

Brewton, John E., and Sara W. Brewton. *Index to Children's Poetry.* suppls. 1954, 1965.

Granger, Edith, ed. *Granger's Index to Poetry.* 5th ed. suppl. 1967.

Deutsch, Babette. *Poetry Handbook: A Dictionary of Terms.*

Let's Get Poetic!—activity list.

Write-on slides.

Art supplies.

Camera and photographic supplies.

Transparencies for sample entries (Subjects, Authors, Titles, First Lines).

Let's Get Poetic!

Choose one of the following activities:

1. Compile an anthology of poetry on a specific theme: wildlife, seasons, holidays, black Americans, cities, etc. Neatly copy each poem.
    a. Use Brewton, John E. *Index to Children's Poetry* and Granger, Edith. *Granger's Index to Poetry.* 5th ed.
    b. Give the source of the poem in correct bibliographic form.
    c. Make an interesting cover for your anthology.

2. Compile an anthology of poetry on a specific theme as suggested above; but instead of writing the poems, record the poems using a cassette recorder.
    a. Practice reading each poem several times before recording.
    b. You may want to add sound effects.
    c. Don't forget to state the source of each poem.

3. Write several poems using one form of poetry: cinquain, haiku, diamante, narrative, or limerick.
    a. Draw illustrations for each poem using a medium of your choice: watercolor, pen and ink, pencil.
    b. Combine into a booklet.

4. Choose poems you like from many sources. Illustrate each poem by designing write-on slides or by taking photographs (slides).
    a. Select and record background music.
    b. Record poems.
    c. Show production to class.

5. Write a poem or select one from a book of poems.
    a. Design a wall hanging.
    b. Use your best calligraphy to record the poem.

6. You may select another activity but you must present a written statement describing the activity to the library media specialist for approval.

Methods:

The teacher will:

1. Plan the unit with the library media specialist.
2. Divide responsibilities.
3. Explain the objectives to the students.
4. Use selections from the sound filmstrips *Understanding Poetry* and *A Pocketful of Poetry* to review poetic forms.
5. Read poems to illustrate various forms.
6. Let students practice writing such forms as haiku, diamante, tanka, cinquain, and limericks.
7. Schedule classes in the library media center.
8. Accompany class to the library media center and assist students with activities.
9. Grade and evaluate activities with library media specialist.

The library media specialist will:

1. Review use of poetry indexes.
2. Prepare transparencies of sample entries for *Subjects, Authors, Titles,* and *First Lines.*
3. Have a collection of poetry books on reserve. Allow students to spend one period reading at least ten poems.
4. Prepare Let's Get Poetic!–list of activities.
5. Distribute list of activities and discuss with students.
6. Let each student choose one activity.
7. Assist students with use of poetry indexes and location of poems, if necessary.
8. Give technical assistance as needed.
9. Grade and evaluate activities with the teacher.

The students will:

1. Review poetic forms.
2. Practice writing poetry using various forms.
3. Review skills for using a poetry index.
4. Select and read at least ten poems.
5. Choose an activity from Let's Get Poetic! list.
6. Complete activity.

Evaluative Criteria: The students will select and read at least ten poems and will successfully complete an activity.

LESSON 6

Title: Literary Literature.

Overview: The purpose of this unit is to assist students in using important reference books in the field of literature.

Library Media Skills Objectives:

Determine the most appropriate reference for a particular purpose.

Use information in preface, foreword, and notes to locate and interpret information.

Identify the organization of the content of a particular reference.

Use guide words to locate appropriate page.

Interpret information.

Performance Objective: Given instruction in the use of reference books in the field of literature and given worksheets, the students will use the assigned reference books to answer questions.

Subject Area: Language Arts.

Learning Strategy: Lecture, discussion, demonstration, practice.

Resources:

Harvey, Paul, and Dorothy Eagle, eds. *Oxford Companion to English Literature.*

Spiller, Robert E., ed. *Literary History of the United States.*

Gassner, John and Edward Quinn, eds. *Reader's Encyclopedia of World Drama.*

Deutsch, Babette. *Poetry Handbook: A Dictionary of Terms.*

Brewton, John E., and Sara W. Brewton. *Index to Children's Poetry.* suppls. 1 and 2.

Bartlett, John. *Bartlett's Familiar Quotations.*

Brussell, Eugene. *Dictionary of Quotable Definitions.*

Benet, William. *The Reader's Encyclopedia.*

Brewer, E. C. *Brewer's Dictionary of Phrase & Fable.*

Bahle, Bruce. *The Home Book of American Quotations.*

Tripp, Rhoda, ed. *The International Thesaurus of Quotations.*

Important Reference Books in the Field of Literature—Worksheets (see pages 194-199).

Transparencies of sample pages (Index, Guide Words, Key to Symbols, etc.).

(Text continues on page 200.)

Important Reference Books in the Field of Literature

Group 1

A. Literary References
The Oxford Companion to English Literature.
Literary History of the United States.
Reader's Encyclopedia of World Drama.

Identify the following:
1. Beauty and the Beast.
2. Dark Ages.
3. Ernest Hemingway, *The Old Man and the Sea.*
4. Romeo and Juliet.

B. Poetry
Deutsch, Babette. *Poetry Handbook.*
Brewton, John, and Sara W. Brewton, *Index to Children's Poetry,* Second Supplement.

Identify the following:
1. Nonsense verse.
2. onomatopoeia.
3. "blind love" written by _____
    located in _____ (name of book).
4. "Mending Wall" by Robert Frost is located in _____.
    (name of book)

C. Quotations
Bartlett, John. *Bartlett's Familiar Quotations.*
Brussell, Eugene. *Dictionary of Quotable Definitions.*

Identify the author and work in which the following statements appear:
1. "As innocent as a new-laid egg."
2. "Child! do not throw this book about; Refrain from the unholy pleasure of cutting all the pictures out! Preserve it as your chiefest treasure."
3. "We always like those who admire us; we do not always like those whom we admire."
4. Conscience—"the voice of your neighbor."
5. Bore—"One who keeps his conversation hohumming."

D. Literature Dictionaries and Encyclopedias.
Benet, William. *The Reader's Encyclopedia.*
Brewer's Dictionary of Phrase & Fable.

Find the meaning or background of the following:
1. beauty sleep.
2. hugger-mugger.
3. mealy-mouthed.
4. jay-walker.
5. Pandora's box.

Important Reference Books in the Field of Literature

Group 2

A.   Literary References.
The Oxford Companion to English Literature.
Literary History of the United States.
Reader's Encyclopedia of World Drama.

Identify the following:
1.   Pooh-Bah.
2.   The House That Jack Built.
3.   Three important short writings of Abraham Lincoln are: The Letter to_____ , the Gettysburg_____ , and the _____ Inaugural.
4.   pantomime.

B.   Poetry
Deutsch, Babette. *Poetry Handbook.*
Brewton, John, and Sara W. Brewton. *Index to Children's Poetry.* Second supplement.

Identify the following:
1.   blank verse.
2.   epitaph.
3.   Give the author and title of a poem about "Hallowe'en."
4.   Alfred Noyes, "The Highwayman" located in_____ .
        (name of book)

C.   Quotations
Bartlett, John. *Bartlett's Familiar Quotations.*
Brussell, Eugene. *Dictionary of Quotable Definitions.*

Identify the author and work in which the following statements appear:
1.   "A tale without love is like beef without mustard: an insipid dish."
2.   "Life is a garment we continually alter, but which never seems to fit."
3.   "Mad, bad, and dangerous to know."
4.   Grass—"The green stuff that wilts on the lawn and thrives in the garden."
5.   Candy—"A universal food; it speaks all languages."

D.   Literature Dictionaries and Encyclopedias.
Benet, William. *The Reader's Encyclopedia.*
Brewer's Dictionary of Phrase and Fable.

Find the meaning or background of the following phrases and sayings:
1.   a scrap of paper.
2.   Four Freedoms.
3.   Rolling Stones.
4.   Swan Song.
5.   rain check.

Important Reference Books in the Field of Literature

Group 3

A. Quotations

Bartlett, John. *Bartlett's Familiar Quotations.*

Brussell, Eugene. *Dictionary of Quotable Definitions.*

Identify the author and work in which the following statements appear:

1. Kangaroo—"An animal that carries its brood in a snood."
2. Hermit—"Anyone without an automobile."
3. "Two heads are better than one."
4. "Fools rush in where angels fear to tread."
5. "Do not wait for the last judgment. It takes place every day."

B. Literature Dictionaries and Encyclopedias.

Benet, William. *The Reader's Encyclopedia.*

Brewer's Dictionary of Phrase and Fable.

Find the meaning or background of the following phrases and sayings:

1. Flying Dutchman.
2. dark horse.
3. Camelot.
4. cake-walk.
5. Mutt and Jeff.

C. Literary References.

The Oxford Companion to English Literature.

Literary History of the United States.

Reader's Encyclopedia of World Drama.

Identify the following:

1. Witwould.
2. Sword-dance.
3. Benjamin Franklin's Almanac, *Poor Richard*, was famous _____ _____.
4. Playboy of the Western World.

D. Poetry.

Deutsch, Babette. *Poetry Handbook.*

Brewton, John, and Sara W. Brewton. *Index to Children's Poetry*, First Supplement.

Identify the following:

1. fable.
2. epic.
3. "Fog" by Carl Sandburg located in _____ .
   (name of book)
4. Complete: "Bird-brain _____ ."
   Written by _____ .

Important Reference Books in the Field of Literature

Group 4

A. Literary References
    The Oxford Companion to English Literature.
    Literary History of the United States.
    Reader's Encyclopedia of World Drama.

    Identify the following:
    1. Yankee Doodle.
    2. Romeo and Juliet.
    3. The place that inspired Herman Melville to write *Omoo.*
    4. Noh.

B. Poetry.
    Deutsch, Babette. *Poetry Handbook.*
    Brewton, John, and Sara W. Brewton. *Index to Children's Poetry*, Second Supplement.

    Identify the following:
    1. pastoral.
    2. Muse.
    3. Give the author and name of a poem about RAINBOWS.
    4. "Stopping By Woods on a Snowy Evening" by Robert Frost located in
        _____.
        (name of book)

C. Quotations.
    Bohle, Bruce. *The Home Book of American Quotations.*
    Tripp, Rhoda. *The International Thesaurus of Quotations.*

    Identify the author and work in which the following statements appear:
    1. "The way to a man's heart is through his stomach."
    2. "Oh! how I hate to get up in the morning."
    3. "Worry, the interest paid by those who borrow trouble."
    4. "One of the signs of passing youth is the birth of a sense of fellowship with other human beings."
    5. "I say, when there are spats, kiss and make up before the day is done and live to fight another day."

D. Literature Dictionaries and Encyclopedias.
    Benet, William. *The Reader's Encyclopedia.*
    Brewer's Dictionary of Phrase and Fable.

    Find the meaning or background of the following:
    1. "Otium cum dignitate."
    2. Puss in Boots.
    3. goody-goody.
    4. sour grapes.
    5. clodhopper.

Important Reference Books in the Field of Literature

Group 5

A. Literary References
The Oxford Companion to English Literature.
Literary History of the United States.
Reader's Encyclopedia of World Drama.

Identify the following:
1. Santa Claus.
2. Swiss Family Robinson.
3. The "temperance movement" inspired Timothy Shay Arthur to write _____ _____.
4. *Our Town.*

B. Poetry.
Deutsch, Babette. *Poetry Handbook.*
Brewton, John, and Sara W. Brewton. *Index to Children's Poetry,* Second Supplement.

Identify the following:
1. vers libre.
2. satire.
3. "A Mermaid Song" written by_____
     located in _____ .
     (name of book)
4. Rudyard Kipling, "The Camel's Hump" located in_____.
     (name of book)

C. Quotations.
Bohle, Bruce. *The Home Book of American Quotations.*
Tripp, Rhoda. *The International Thesaurus of Quotations.*

Identify the author and work in which the following statements appear:
1. "It is wiser being good than bad."
2. "The earth is a beehive; we all enter by the same door but live in different cells."
3. "When a dog bites a man that is not news, but when a man bites a dog that is news."
4. "There will never be a civilized country until we expend more money for books than we do for chewing-gum."
5. "It don't cost nothing to be a gentleman."

D. Literature Dictionaries and Encyclopedias.
Benet, William. *The Reader's Encyclopedia.*
Brewer's Dictionary of Phrase and Fable.

Find the meaning or background of the following phrases and sayings:
1. fourth estate.
2. humble pie.
3. liberal arts.
4. the web of Penelope.
5. R. I. P.

Important Reference Books in the Field of Literature

Group 6

A. Literary References
   The Oxford Companion to English Literature.
   Literary History of the United States.
   Reader's Encyclopedia of World Drama.

   Identify the following:
   1. Leprechaun.
   2. *Midsummer Night's Dream.*
   3. Radio: the master of all radio orators was_____ .
   4. *The Hairy Ape.*

B. Poetry.
   Deutsch, Babette. *Poetry Handbook.*
   Brewton, John, and Sara W. Brewton. *Index to Children's Poetry.*

   Identify the following:
   1. haiku.
   2. parallelism.
   3. Complete "If a pig _____"
      written by _____ located in_____
      _____ .
            (name of book)
   4. Alfred Lord Tennyson, "The Charge of the Light Brigade" located in _____
      _____ .
            (name of book)

C. Quotations
   Bohle, Bruce. *The Home Book of American Quotations.*
   Tripp, Rhoda. *The International Thesaurus of Quotations.*

   Identify the author and work in which the following statements appear:
   1. "He that falls in love with himself will have no rivals."
   2. "Wisdom is the child of experience."
   3. "There is no cure for birth or death save to enjoy the interval."
   4. "Poverty is no disgrace to a man, but it is confoundedly inconvenient."
   5. "If the blind lead the blind, both shall fall into the ditch."

D. Literature Dictionaries and Encyclopedias.
   Benet, William. *The Reader's Encyclopedia.*
   Brewer's Dictionary of Phrase and Fable.

   Find the meaning or background in the following phrases and sayings:
   1. Don't play the giddy goat.
   2. the old lady of Threadneedle Street.
   3. cum laude.
   4. Knight of the pencil.
   5. Another man's shoes.

Methods:

The teacher will:

1. Plan with the library media specialist for the lesson to be taught after the students have completed a literature unit that requires a literary report.
2. Schedule the library media specialist to come to the classroom.
3. Reinforce the skills taught as the students use the reference books for their literary report.
4. Evaluate the unit with the library media specialist.

The library media specialist will:

1. Write questions and prepare worksheets for Groups 1-6.
2. Make copies of sample pages (Index, Guide Words, Key to Symbols, etc.) from each reference book listed on the worksheet. Make a transparency of each page.
3. Put the reference books listed in the resources on a cart for reserve use in the classroom.
4. Go to the classroom and give a brief overview of each reference book on the cart.
5. Use transparencies to demonstrate how to use an index to locate a poem or a quotation.
6. Divide students into six groups.
7. Give each group a set of questions.
8. Instruct the group members to work together to answer the questions.
9. After all groups have completed the assignment, ask students to share answers with the entire class.
10. Leave books in the classroom for students to use for their literary report.
11. Evaluate the unit with the teacher.

The students will:

1. Learn how to use special reference books by taking part in the demonstration lesson by the library media specialist.
2. Work with a group to answer questions on the worksheet Important Reference Books in the Field of Literature.
3. Use reference books in preparing literary report.

Evaluative Criteria: The students will successfully answer the questions given to their group by using the assigned reference books.

LESSON 7

Title: The Britannica 3: Pro, Micro, Macro.

Overview: The purpose of this lesson is to introduce the *Britannica 3 Encyclopaedia* to students to help them effectively use the *Propaedia*, the *Micropaedia*, the *Macropaedia*, and the Library Guide to locate information on the history and foundations of mathematics and the ancient Greek civilization. The lesson is designed for advanced or gifted students in mathematics.

Library Media Skills Objectives:

Use specified reference materials to develop and support research.

Select relevant material from an encyclopedia index.

Utilize resources to organize and prepare a written report.

Evaluate material based on authority.

Performance Objective: Given a pretest on the *Britannica 3 Encyclopaedia*, the students will use the *Propaedia*, the *Micropaedia* and the *Macropaedia* to locate information on a topic of their choice related to the history and foundation of mathematics or ancient Greek civilization. They will take notes and utilize information to prepare a written report. They will take a written posttest and achieve at least 85% on the test.

Subject Area: Mathematics.

Learning Strategy: Lecture, practice.

Resources:

Britannica 3 Encyclopaedia set

Sound Filmstrip: *How to Use Britannica 3 Encyclopaedia.* Encyclopaedia Britannica Educational Corporation.

How Britannica 3 Helps Teachers and Students. (Study Guide) Encyclopaedia Britannica Educational Corporation.

Library Guide to Encyclopaedia Britannica.

Pretest, posttest (see page 202).

Transparencies (see page 203).

Methods:

The teacher will:

1. Introduce the lesson by explaining the purpose of the lesson, which is to provide an historical background of the foundations of mathematics and an appreciation for the intellectual contributions of the ancient Greek civilization.
2. Plan the research activities with the library media specialist.
3. Schedule classes in the library media center.

(Text continues on page 204.)

Test for Encyclopaedia Britannica 3

1. Briefly explain the purpose of the following sections:

    Micropaedia:

    Macropaedia:

    Propaedia:

2. Define these reference terms:

    see _____

    see also _____

    Cf _____

    q.v._____

    related entries_____

3. Identify the parts of the following notations:

    13:942e _____

    11:31h _____

    14:262f passim to 269h _____

    VI:373a _____

4. Draw a chart and label it to signify the location of information on each page.

5. How can you determine that the articles in the *Macropaedia* and *Propaedia* were written by competent authorities?

Transparencies

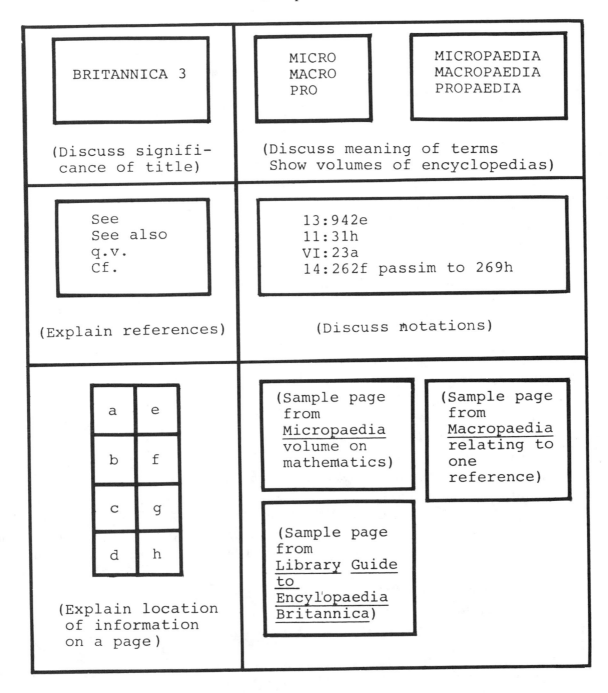

7. Give examples of topics to read in the Propaedia to
   begin research:

Methods (cont'd.)

4. Assist the library media specialist with the discussion on the use of the *Britannica 3* after the introductory lesson by the library media specialist.

5. Review and approve student-selected topics for reports.

6. Assist with research.

7. Grade written report: Include grade from posttest given by library media specialist.

The library media specialist will:

1. Prepare a pretest for the *Britannica 3*.

2. Introduce the lesson by asking students to take the pretest.

3. Ask if there are any students who think they correctly answered all questions.

4. If so, collect those papers and check answers.

5. Ask the rest of the students to view the filmstrip *How to Use Britannica 3* to find answers to the questions on the pretest.

6. Prepare transparencies to use with lecture.

7. Give examples of topics to read in the *Propaedia* to begin research.
   History and Foundations of Mathematics.
   Greek and Hellenistic Mathematics.
   Numerals and Numerals System.
   Greek Numerals.
   Greek Geometry.

8. Show the *Micropaedia* volume on mathematics.
   Show transparency of one page.
   Explain the notations and references.

9. Show the *Macropaedia* volume relating to one reference.
   Show transparency of one page.

10. Show the *Library Guide to Encyclopaedia Britannica*.
    Show transparency of one page.
    Discuss the use of this guide as an additional resource.

11. Discuss the significance of the initials in the *Macropaedia* articles and the author's name in the *Propaedia*. Select one or two names and find information about them in other reference sources.

12. Assist students with research.

13. Ask students to take a posttest after students complete written reports.

14. Use the pretest questions for the posttest.

15. Grade the posttest.

16. Evaluate the lesson with the teacher.

Methods (cont'd.)

The students will:

1. Take a pretest on the *Britannica 3.*
2. View filmstrip *How to Use Britannica 3.*
3. Listen to lecture and participate in discussion.
4. Have teacher approve topic for research.
5. Use *Propaedia, Micropaedia,* and *Macropaedia* to locate information on chosen topic.
6. Write report.
7. Take posttest.

Evaluative Criteria: The students will use the *Propaedia, Micropaedia,* and *Macropaedia* to locate information on their chosen topic, write a report, and achieve at least 85% on a written posttest.

LESSON 8

Title: Bon Appétit!

Overview: The purpose of this unit is to help students increase their French cooking vocabulary by playing the game *Bon Appétit!* by Gessler Publishers and by preparing a French dish.

Library Media Skills Objectives:

Use a foreign language dictionary.

Use card catalog.

Use an index.

Performance Objective: Given the game *Bon Appétit!*, a French-English dictionary, and access to cookbooks, the students will play *Bon Appétit!*, they will define twenty French cooking terms, and they will prepare a French dish.

Subject Area: French.

Learning Strategy: Game, practice.

Resources:

Game: *Bon Appétit!* (3 games).*

Dictionaries: French-English and English-French.

Cookbooks: dePomiane, Edouard. *French Cooking in Ten Minutes.*
Macdonald, Lyn. *French Cooking without Tears.*
Howe, Robin. *French Cookery.*

Methods:

The teacher will:

1.   Check with the library media specialist concerning availability of resources well in advance of unit.
2.   Plan unit with library media specialist.
3.   Introduce the unit and explain objectives to students.
4.   Divide students into groups to play game *Bon Appétit!* Explain rules.
5.   Prepare a list of twenty French cooking terms. Ask students to define terms from the vocabulary they learned by playing the game or by using a dictionary.
6.   Allow small groups of students to go to the library media center to locate cookbooks with French cuisine.
7.   Ask students to work in small groups to prepare a French dish. (This may be coordinated with a home economics food lab.)
8.   Plan a field trip to a French restaurant as a culminating activity.

---

*The *Bon Appétit!* games are available from Gessler Publishing Co., Inc., 220 E. Twenty-third St., New York, NY 10010.

Methods (cont'd.)

The library media specialist will:

1. Reserve at least three *Bon Appétit!* games for use in the French class.
2. Check cookbooks for recipes of French dishes.
3. Assist groups in locating recipes as needed.
4. Accompany class to French restaurant.

The students will:

1. Play the game *Bon Appétit!*
2. Define French cooking terms.
3. Locate cookbooks of French cuisine.
4. Prepare a French dish.
5. Share food with class members.
6. Eat lunch at a French restaurant.

Evaluative Criteria: The students will play *Bon Appétit!*, define twenty French cooking terms, and prepare a French dish.

LESSON 9

Title: To Copy or Not to Copy.

Overview: The purpose of this lesson is to inform students about the meaning and purpose of the United States Copyright Law, P. L. 94-533, and to suggest guidelines for student use of copyrighted materials.

Library Media Skills Objectives:

Locate and interpret copyright symbol.

Observe copyright laws.

Performance Objective: Given information on the meaning and purpose of the United States Copyright Law, P. L. 94-533, the students will complete a test, To Copy or Not to Copy, to determine their understanding of the lawful use of copyrighted material.

Subject Area: Social Studies.

Learning Strategy: Discussion, reading, practice.

Resources:

Federal Copyright Statute, Public Law 94-533. Obtain from Copyright Office, Library of Congress, Washington, D. C. 20559.

Book: Gary, Charles. *The New Copyright Law and Education.* Educational Research Service.

Articles: "Copyright, Media and the School Librarian." *School Media Quarterly* (Spring 1978): A-P.

Rothenberg, Stanley. "Copyright." *Encyclopedia Americana.* vol. 7 (1981): 772-776.

Transparencies.

To Copy or Not to Copy—Test.

Methods:

The teacher will:

1.   Plan the lesson with the library media specialist.
2.   Include the lesson as a part of the unit on law.
3.   Include questions from the lesson on the unit test.
4.   Schedule the class in the library media center.

To Copy or Not to Copy

Under Public Law 94-533, the United States Copyright Law, students may or may not lawfully use copyrighted material in the following ways: (State **Yes** or **No**.)

_____1. Copy a photograph from a magazine for use in social studies report.

_____2. Make a single copy on a reader-printer from microform.

_____3. Perform musical work at school dance when compensation is paid to performers.

_____4. Use opaque projector to trace a single map for class project.

_____5. Use a paragraph in direct quotes from a reference book including a notice of copyright.

_____6. Make an off-air recording of a commercial television program and bring the video tape to school to show to a class.

_____7. Copy a record album belonging to a friend.

_____8. Make a single copy of a cartoon for use on a poster for language arts class.

_____9. Use a sound recording owned by the library media center as background music for a slide/tape class project.

_____10. Perform a play for which a royalty has been paid.

_____11. Copy a computer software program from the library media center collection for personal use on home computer.

_____12. Record stories, poems, or songs in the public domain.

_____13. Copy a small portion of a radio program to use as an introduction to a speech.

_____14. Use a recording as background music for a student video production to be performed at a state film festival.

_____15. Make slides from book of photographs after obtaining permission from copyright owner.

Answer Key: 1 yes, 2 yes, 3 no, 4 yes, 5 yes, 6 no, 7 no, 8 yes, 9 yes, 10 yes, 11 no, 12 yes, 13 yes, 14 no, 15 yes.

Methods (cont'd.)

The library media specialist will:

1. Have the primary responsibility for teaching the lesson.
2. Make transparencies using primary typewriter. List "Exclusive Rights of Copyright Owners" and "Limitations on the Exclusive Rights of Copyright Owners."
3. Introduce the lesson by asking students to brainstorm ideas about the purpose and use of copyright laws.
   - List students' ideas on transparencies.
   - Incorporate students' ideas into discussion.
   - Give a brief history of copyright laws.
   - Summarize Public Law 94-533. Use transparencies made with primary typewriter.
   - Discuss criteria for *fair use:*
     purpose, type of material, amount to be copied in relation to the whole, financial effect on owner of copyright.
   - Define:
     Public Domain.
     Plagiarism.
     Royalties.
   - Discuss penalties for infringement of copyrighted materials.
   - Show samples of requests for permisssion to use copyrighted materials.
4. Ask students to take test To Copy or Not to Copy.
5. Let students check their answers as each question is discussed.
6. Ask students to put their corrected copy of the test in their school handbook.
7. Evaluate lesson with the social studies teacher.

The students will:

1. Brainstorm ideas about copyright laws.
2. Discuss the meaning and purpose of Public Law 94-533.
3. Complete the test To Copy or Not to Copy.
4. Correct and discuss answers to the test.
5. Include corrected copy of test in school handbook.

Evaluative Criteria: The students will take a test, To Copy or Not to Copy, and will check the test to ensure that all answers are correct.

LESSON 10

Title: Where to Go...

Overview: The purpose of this lesson is to tell students where to go to find information for a science fair project. The lesson can serve as a review of library media center information sources. It should be used with advanced science students.

Library Media Skills Objectives:

Locate resources using the card catalog.

Locate print and nonprint materials for specific information.

Use indexes to locate information on a given topic.

Use dictionaries, almanacs, encyclopedias, handbooks, manuals, directories.

Performance Objective: Given a review of library media center information sources, the students will locate and utilize data for a written presentation to accompany a science fair project.

Subject Area: Science.

Learning Strategy: Lecture/discussion, practice, report.

Resources:

Dictionaries.

Card catalog.

Manuals.

Directories.

Periodical indexes.

Almanacs.

Encyclopedias.

Handbooks.

Indexes.

Statistical abstracts.

Yearbooks.

Vertical file.

Newspapers.

Magazines.

Databank.

Organizations.

Book: Whitney, David. *First Book of Facts and How to Find Them.*

Resources (cont'd.)

Game: *Search and Research—A Library Skills Game*. Educational Activities.

Task Cards: *Information Fast!* Educational Insights.

Leaflet: *A Student's Guide to Library Reference Materials*. Facts on File, Inc.

Filmstrip: *Choosing the Medium*. Encyclopaedia Britannica Educational Corp.

Movie (16-mm): *The Reference Section*. Barr Films. (optional)

Transparencies—using primary type (see pages 213 and 214).

Methods:

The teacher will:

1. Plan the lesson with the library media specialist.
2. Inform the students that for their science fair project they must complete a written presentation to accompany their science fair project.
3. Check each student's written proposal for the science fair project.
4. Explain the objective.
5. State that the library media specialist will review information sources and assist with location of information.
6. Remind students that they may also use the learning center in the science room, which gives detailed information on science fair projects.
7. Schedule classes in the library media center.

The library media specialist will:

1. Introduce the lesson by showing slides of the winning entries in last year's science fair.
2. Ask the students to name some of the steps that were used to produce these projects.
3. Emphasize the importance of collecting, analyzing, interpreting, drawing conclusions, and organizing data.
4. Use transparencies to review library media center information sources.
    Have a cart of materials and show them with the transparencies.
5. Set up several learning centers with print and nonprint resources for use by students who need guidance (see list under resources).
6. Make a student packet of information "Where to Go..." to distribute after presentation.
7. Assist students in locating resources.
8. Evaluate lesson with science teacher.

The students will:

1. View slides of winning entries in the science fair.
2. Discuss some possible procedures, techniques, and research skills that students used in preparing their science fair projects.
3. View, listen, and think about ideas from transparencies on "Where to Go..."
4. Visit learning centers for help in using specific resources.
5. Locate and utilize print and nonprint materials for written presentation to accompany science fair project.
6. Make a bibliography.
7. Complete science fair project.

Evaluative Criteria: The students will locate and utilize data in a written presentation to accompany a science fair project.

Transparencies

WHERE TO GO...	TO LOCATE INFORMATION

CHECK THESE FIRST! CARD CATALOG VERTICAL FILE DATABASE	CAN'T FIND SUBJECT HEADINGS? TRY: SEARS LIST OF SUBJECT HEADINGS DEWEY'S RELATIVE INDEX FOR: RELATED TOPICS

NEED REFERENCE HELP? USE: GUIDE TO REFERENCE BOOKS BOOKS IN PRINT	EXCELLENT SOURCES: GENERAL ENCYCLOPEDIAS SCIENCE ENCYCLOPEDIAS YEARBOOKS DIRECTORIES

REMEMBER TO CHECK: MICROFORMS COMPUTER SOFTWARE FILMS FILMSTRIPS SLIDES RECORDINGS	DON'T FORGET: ALMANACS DICTIONARIES MANUALS HANDBOOKS YELLOW PAGES— TELEPHONE DIRECTORY

OF SPECIAL NOTE:

NATIONAL GEOGRAPHIC INDEX
VAN NOSTRAND'S SCIENTIFIC
    ENCYCLOPEDIA
COMPTON'S DICTIONARY OF
    NATURAL SCIENCE

NEED CURRENT INFORMATION?
USE:

READERS' GUIDE TO
    PERIODICAL LITERATURE
FACTS ON FILE
DAILY NEWSPAPER
CURRENT MAGAZINES
TELEVISION NEWS

BIOGRAPHICAL SOURCES:
USE:

WEBSTER'S BIOGRAPHICAL DICT.
CURRENT BIOGRAPHY
WHO'S WHO IN AMERICA
INDEX TO SCIENTISTS
NEW CENTURY CYCLOPEDIA OF
    NAMES
ASIMOV'S BIOGRAPHICAL ENCYCLO.

CAN'T FIND THE RIGHT WORDS?
USE:

GENERAL DICTIONARIES
    ABRIDGED
    UNABRIDGED
SCIENTIFIC DICTIONARIES
THESAURUS

ORGANIZATIONS:

NATIONAL SCIENCE FOUNDATION
NASA
NATIONAL WILDLIFE FEDERATION

OTHER SOURCES TO CHECK:

PUBLIC LIBRARY
COLLEGE LIBRARY
SPECIALISTS IN
    COMMUNITY

ASK YOUR FRIENDLY
LIBRARY MEDIA
SPECIALIST!

LESSON 11

Title: Building Blocks.

Overview: The purpose of this unit is to assist students in identifying desirable characteristics of books, magazines, and television programs for preschool children. It is designed to be used with a home economics child care unit.

Library Media Skills Objectives:

Select print and nonprint materials appropriate to ability level.

Select print and nonprint material based on specific criteria.

Performance Objective: Given criteria for evaluating books, magazines, and television programs for preschool children, the students will evaluate at least three books, two magazines, and one television program.

Subject Area: Home Economics: Child Care Unit.

Learning Strategy: Lecture, reading, audiovisual instruction, practice.

Resources:

Evaluation forms (see page 216).

Books: Duvoisin, Roger. *A for the Ark.*

Brown, Marcia. *Once a Mouse.*

Yashima, Taro. *Umbrella.*

Dr. Seuss. *The Cat in the Hat Came Back.*

Freeman, Don. *A Pocket for Corduroy.*

Wildsmith, Brian. *1, 2, 3.*

Ets, Marie. *Just Me.*

Minarik, Elsa. *Little Bear.*

Anno, Mitsumara. *The King's Flower.*

Magazines: *Jack & Jill.*

Highlights.

Sesame Street.

TV Guide.

Methods:

The teacher will:

1. Plan the unit with the library media specialist.
2. Introduce the unit by discussing the purpose and performance objective.
3. Schedule the lesson to be taught by the library media specialist in the library media center.
4. Assign learning activities as a follow-up to the lesson.

Comic Book or Magazine Evaluation

Title:

Publisher:

Cost:

Rate the following characteristics:

	Excellent	Good	Fair
Content meets needs and interests of preschool child.			
Illustrations appropriate and pleasing.			
Advertisements of high quality.			
Content avoids stereotyping.			
Paper of good quality.			

Book Evaluation

Title:

Author:

Publisher:

Cost:

Rate the following:

	Excellent	Good	Fair
Book well written.			
Content contributes to child's appreciation and understanding of world.			
Characters convincing and credible.			
Illustrations reflect spirit of the book.			
Illustrations pleasing and satisfying.			
Print clear and appropriate to age group.			
Author avoids stereotyping.			

Television Program Evaluation

Title:

Producer:

Rate the following:

	Excellent	Good	Fair
Content understandable to child.			
Language appropriate for child.			
Program avoids stereotyping.			
Content stimulating to child's imagination.			
Values expressed in children's terms.			
Content and subject worthy of interest.			
Visuals pleasing and noteworthy.			
Time convenient for child to view.			
Number of commercial interruptions.			
Commercials of high quality and interest to children.			

Methods (cont'd.)

5. Lead students in discussion of completed learning activities.
6. Evaluate unit with library media specialist.

The library media specialist will:

1. Prepare evaluation forms for judging magazines, books, and television programs.
2. Select books and magazines (appropriate for preschool children) to use in book talk. Borrow books from elementary media center or public library.
3. Copy television program for children from state ITV broadcasts, which allow duplication for educational use.
4. Give book talk on judging books for preschool children. Discuss evaluative criteria. Include the following:
    Types of books—Picture Books, Mother Goose, Nursery Rhymes, ABC, Counting, Fairy Tales, Story Books.
    Subject Matter—Familiar or fanciful, creative, true to human nature or to nature of animals, good plot, adequate characterization.
    Theme—Simple concepts.
    Language—Stimulating; use of humor, repetition, and rhyme; expressive vocabulary.
    Illustrations—Imaginative, express spirit and meaning of story.
5. Show video taped children's program. Lead discussion on the suitability of the program based on the Television Program Evaluation form.
6. Evaluate the unit with the home economics teacher.

The students will:

1. Participate in discussions led by teacher and library media specialist.
2. Listen to book talk and view video tape of children's program.
3. Read children's books and magazines.
4. Complete assigned activities of evaluating books, magazines, and television programs.
5. Do optional activity for extra credit.
    Make a picture book or write a story using criteria from Book Evaluation form.

Evaluative Criteria: The students will successfully evaluate three books, two magazines, and one television program for preschool children.

LESSON 12

Title: "Singing the Black Bug Blues."

Overview: The purpose of this lesson is to give students an opportunity to work independently on a science project based on their own interests. One example of a research project is a slide/tape presentation on "How to Make an Insect Collection." The guidance counselor will provide the instruction and guidance in photography.

Library Media Skills Objectives:

Interpret specialized reference materials to develop and support research.

Use organizational skills to produce a multimedia presentation.

Organize to show sequence.

Produce a media presentation that contains specific subject matter.

Performance Objective: Given an independent study guide, the students will identify a topic of inquiry, locate and evaluate resources, interpret specialized reference materials, and organize and produce a multimedia presentation.

Subject Area: Science.

Learning Strategy: Discussion, project.

Resources:

Books: Callahan, Philip. *Insect Behavior.*

Hutchins, Ross. *The Bug Clan.*

Hutchins, Ross. *Insects and Their Young.*

Borrar, Donald J., and Richard E. White. *A Field Guide to the Insects of America North of Mexico.*

Patent, Dorothy. *How Insects Communicate.*

Kit: *Insects: How They Help Us.* National Geographic.

Film loop: *Insect Collecting.* Ealing.

35-mm Camera, Film, Processing Mailers.

Independent Study Guide for Science Classes. (See page 219.)

Methods:

The teacher will:

1. Explain the Independent Study Guide for Science Classes.
2. Discuss requirements and expectations.
3. Review and approve independent research topics such as "How to Make an Insect Collection."
4. Meet with the library media specialist and guidance counselor to plan strategies for working with students who are on independent study.

Independent Study Guide for Science Classes

You may work independently or in small groups.

1. Identify a topic for study.

2. Pose questions of inquiry related to topics.

3. Hypothesize answers.

4. Carry out an investigation or research to verify hypothesized answers.

5. Plan a media presentation to effectively share your investigation.

6. Organize and produce a multimedia presentation.

Methods (cont'd.)

5. Meet with student or students at a scheduled time to discuss and review activities.
6. Evaluate the multimedia presentation with the library media specialist and guidance counselor.

The library media specialist will:

1. Meet with student or students to determine media-related needs.
2. Assist with obtaining and utilizing resources.
3. Guide students in planning slide/tape production "How to Make an Insect Collection."
   - Prepare a storyboard.
   - Take photographs.
   - Write script.
   - Select or create musical background.
4. Work with guidance counselor who will give instruction in photography.
5. Evaluate multimedia presentation with teacher, guidance counselor, and students.

The guidance counselor will:

1. Give instruction in photography: use of 35-mm camera, composition techniques, and special effects.
2. Evaluate multimedia presentation with teacher, library media specialist, and students.

The students will:

1. Select topic for research such as "How to Make an Insect Collection."
2. Meet with the science teacher, guidance counselor, and library media specialist to discuss topic and strategies.
3. Locate and utilize resources:
   filmstrips, books, film loop.
4. Plan storyboard.
5. Get special instruction and guidance from the guidance counselor on photographic techniques.
6. Take slides during collection, storing, classifying, mounting, labeling, and organizing of insects.
7. Preview and evaluate slides with guidance counselor and library media specialist.
8. Take additional slides, if necessary.
9. Make graphics titles and credits.
10. Organize slide/tape presentation.
11. Tape a narration to accompany slides.
12. Work with teacher to compose and perform original music such as "The Black Bug Blues."
13. View and evaluate.

Evaluative Criteria: The students will select a topic for independent study and will successfully complete a multimedia presentation.

LESSON 13

Title: Let's Communicate!

Overview: The purpose of this unit is to allow students to explore many methods of visual and non-verbal communications. They will select one method of nonverbal communication and will prepare a demonstration exercise.

Library Media Skills Objectives:

Select material appropriate for given purpose.

Utilize information from many sources.

Select media format to communicate ideas.

Performance Objective: Given information on visual and nonverbal communications, the students will select one method of nonverbal communication and will prepare a demonstration exercise that will be videotaped and shown to the class.

Subject Area: Language Arts.

Learning Strategy: Demonstration, discussion, role-playing.

Resources:

Dictionaries.

Books: Greene, Laura, and Eva Dicker. *Sign Language.*

Lubell, Winifred, and Cecil Lubell. *Picture Signs & Symbols.*

Helfman, Elizabeth. *Blissymbolics: Speaking without Speech.*

Mortensen, C. David. *Communication.*

Film: *The Gold Rush.* United Artists.

Organizations: National Association of the Deaf, 814 Thayer Ave., Silver Spring, MD 20907.

Methods:

The teacher will:

1. Discuss the purpose of the unit and type of resources needed with the library media specialist.
2. Explain the objectives of the unit to the students.
3. Introduce the unit by asking students to define *communications.* Ask a student to look up the meaning in a dictionary and share with class.
4. Discuss meaning and give examples of verbal communications.
5. Discuss communication *roadblocks* (ordering, judging, diverting, etc.) and *facilitators* (listening, feedback).
6. Ask students to name types of *nonverbal communication* (pantomime, body language, facial expressions, sign language, signals).

Methods (cont'd.)

7. Ask how many students know sign language and would be willing to demonstrate one of the sign language systems.

8. Invite a trained teacher of sign language systems to demonstrate various systems such as: Ameslan (ASL), Manual English, Word/Sound Systems, Rochester Method, and Total Communications. (One class period.)
    Discuss meaning of *hearing impaired* and needs of hearing impaired people.

9. Discuss the importance of feedback in communication through body language and facial expressions.

10. Demonstrate pantomime by telling a story or by viewing Charlie Chaplin in *The Gold Rush.*

11. Divide class into six groups.

12. Instruct each group to select a method of nonverbal communication and to plan a demonstration exercise that will be videotaped and shown to the class.

13. Allow students time to work as a group and time to use the resources in the library media center.

14. Schedule video taping times with the library media specialist.

15. View and evaluate video taped demonstrations with students.

16. Ask students to give feedback.

The library media specialist will:

1. Gather and reserve materials for the unit.

2. Write or call the National Association of the Deaf for resource material.

3. Assist students in locating material.

4. Schedule video taping sessions.

5. Plan for library media student assistants to videotape the demonstration exercises.

6. View and evaluate the video tape with students and the teacher.

The students will:

1. Define *communications.*

2. Give examples of verbal and nonverbal communications.

3. Learn about needs of hearing-impaired people.
    Learn ways of communicating through sign language.

4. Work with a group to plan a demonstration exercise using a method of nonverbal communication (pantomime, body language, facial expressions, signals, sign language).

5. Use resources in the library media center.

6. Make a storyboard of demonstration lesson.

7. Practice and perform demonstrations for video taping.

8. View and evaluate video tape.

Evaluative Criteria: The students will prepare a demonstration exercise using a method of nonverbal communication that will be videotaped and shown to the class.

LESSON 14

Title: Enchanting Fantasy.

Overview: The purpose of this lesson is to introduce students to the enchanting world of fantasy literature to encourage them to read for pleasure and to develop and strengthen their capacity for creative thinking and imaginative response.

Library Media Skills Objectives:

Recognize different types of nonrealistic fiction.

Select reading as a leisure-time activity.

Performance Objectives: Given the characteristics of fantasy literature, the student will list at least three forms of fantasy literature and will cite the unique characteristics of each. The student will select and read at least one book from the reading list. The student will complete a creative project of his or her choice.

Subject Area: Language Arts.

Learning Strategy: Discussion, audiovisual instruction, reading, project.

Resources:

Professional resources:

Books: Bettelheim, Bruno. *The Use of Enchantment: The Meaning and Importance of Fairy Tales.*

Helms, Randel. *Tolkien's World.*

Pamphlets: "The Return of the King." A teacher's guide to fantasy literature. Prime Time School Television, 1980.

Records: "Puff the Magic Dragon." Golden Records.

"Poems and Songs of the Middle Earth." Caedmon.

Poems: "Jabberwocky." From Lewis Carroll, *Through the Looking Glass.*

Films: "The Wizard of Oz." MGM.

Important Authors and Titles in Fantasy—Reading list for students (see page 224).

Methods:

The teacher will:

1. Introduce the genre of fantasy literature giving the unique characteristics of each form.
2. Use poems, records, films, and filmstrips to cite examples.
3. Explain objectives, assignments, and evaluative criteria.
4. Schedule classes in the library media center.
5. Assist students with projects.

Important Authors and Titles of Fantasy

Alexander, Lloyd. *The Book of Three.*
The Cat Who Wished to Be a Man.
The Wizard in the Tree.
Castle of Llyr.
High King.

Babbitt, Natalie. *The Search for Delicious.*

Boston, L. M. *Treasure of Green Knowe.*

Butterworth, Oliver. *The Enormous Egg.*

Cervantes, Miguel. *The Adventures of Don Quixote De La Mancha.*

Cleary, Beverly. *The Mouse and the Motorcycle.*

Cooper, Susan. *The Dark Is Rising.*
The Grey King.
Silver on the Tree.

Garner, Alan. *The Moon of Gomrath.*
The Weirdstone of Brisingamen.

Juster, Norton. *The Phantom Tollbooth.*

Kendall, Carol. *The Gammage Cup.*

Lawson, Robert. *Rabbit Hill.*

Lewis, C. S. *The Lion, the Witch and the Wardrobe.*

Lindgren, Astrid. *Pippi Longstocking.*

L'Engle, Madeleine. *A Wrinkle in Time.*

McKillip, Patricia A. *The Forgotten Beasts of Eld.*
Heir of Sea and Fire.

Merrill, Jean. *The Pushcart War.*

Milne, A. A. *The World of Pooh.*

Nichols, Ruth. *A Walk out of the World.*

Norton, Mary. *Bed Knob and Broomstick.*
The Borrowers.
The Borrowers Afloat.

Picard, Barbara. *The Faun and the Woodcutter's Daughter.*

Selden, George. *The Genie of Sutton Place.*

Thurber, James. *The 13 Clocks.*

Tolkien, J. R. R. *The Hobbit.*
The Lord of the Rings.
The Silmarillion.
The Two Towers.

Travers, P. L. *Mary Poppins.*

White, E. B. *Charlotte's Web.*

Methods (cont'd.)

The library media specialist will:

1. Present book talks: fairy tale, legend, myth, science fiction.
2. Prepare and distribute reading lists.
3. Assist students with projects.

The students will:

1. Listen to the record "Puff the Magic Dragon" and discuss the theme.
2. Read and discuss the poem "Jabberwocky."
3. View films and filmstrips on fantasy literature.
4. Listen to book talks.
5. Select and read a book of fantasy.
6. Create a project. Some examples are:
    Write a fairy tale or myth.
    Compose a song or poem.
    Draw a cartoon.
    Construct a model.
    Create a book of fantastic creatures.
    Design a poster or chart.
    Make a filmstrip.
    Trace a legend.
    Make a diorama.
    Write a character analysis of Darth Vader.
    Compare Superman to the Incredible Hulk.

Evaluative Criteria: The student will successfully complete all activities. The teacher and library media specialist will evaluate the projects according to the following criteria: originality of theme, organization, presentation, general effectiveness.

LESSON 15

Title: The Art of Animation.

Overview: The purpose of this unit is to promote creative expression through the production of an animated movie.

Library Media Skills Objectives:

Select media format to communicate content or ideas.

Define objective.

Write a script.

Prepare a storyboard.

Prepare visuals (graphics).

Shoot a super 8-mm animated movie.

Record background music/or sound effects.

Performance Objective: Given instruction in the steps for planning and producing a super 8-mm animated movie, the students will write a script, prepare visuals, and plan and produce an animated movie.

Subject Area: Art.

Learning Strategy: Demonstration, practice, audiovisual project.

Resources:

Super 8-mm camera and projector.

Editor.

Super 8-mm movie film.

Super 8-mm splices.

Cassette recorder.

Art supplies.

Books: Helfman, Harry. *Making Your Own Movies.*
         Kinsey, Anthony. *How to Make Animated Movies.*
         Laybourne, Kit. *The Animation Book.*

16-mm Movies: *Animation Pie.* Parker Films.
                Claymation. Billy Budd Films.

Methods:

The teacher will:

1. Plan the unit with the library media specialist who will share the teaching responsibilities.
2. Explain the objective to the students.
3. Show the following 16-mm films on animation:
    Animation Pie.
    Claymation.
4. Schedule library media specialist to show student-produced animated movies.
5. Brainstorm ideas for script.
6. Decide on medium: cutouts, clay, etc.
7. Schedule library media specialist to teach steps in producing an animated movie.
8. Assign duties: producer, storyboard, script, background scenery, graphics, clay figures, photography, editing, sound.
9. Supervise graphics and clay modeling.
10. Ask library media specialist to supervise filming.
11. View and evaluate completed super 8-mm animated movie.

The library media specialist will:

1. Plan unit with art teacher.
2. Prepare a timetable for activities.
3. Obtain resources (except art supplies).
4. Show a student-produced animated movie such as "Flop Flops Them All," "The Sea Odyssey," or "Plate Tectonics."
5. Teach steps in producing an animated movie:
    * Get to know camera: focus, exposure, lighting, types of film.
    * State objective.
    * Plan storyboard.
    * Write script.
    * Prepare visuals.
    * Rehearse scenes.
    * Film animated movie.
    * Keep records.
    * Have film processed.
    * Edit.
    * Add sound.
    * View and evaluate.
6. Let students start a practice roll of super 8-mm film to check exposure, lighting, focus.
7. Supervise actual shooting.
    (Set up filming area where camera and visuals will not have to be moved.)
8. Have film processed.
9. Supervise procedures for editing and splicing.

Methods (cont'd.)

10. Supervise recording of background music and/or sound effects: Remind students about the copyright law.

11. View and evaluate.

The students will:

1. View 16-mm movies on animation techniques.

2. View student-produced animated movies.

3. Brainstorm ideas for production.

4. Decide on content, theme, and purpose. For example:

    Let's make an animated movie, using clay models, to illustrate how students abuse chairs at school. The chairs can come to life and abuse students. The moral is "Do unto chairs, as chairs would do unto you."

5. Learn techniques for producing an animated movie.

6. State objective, prepare storyboard, write script.

7. Decide on title, for example, "Don't Sit on Me."

8. Prepare scenery, title, and credits.

9. Model clay figures.

10. Set up camera and background for animation.

11. Rehearse scenes.

12. Film animated movie, paying careful attention to detail.

13. Take care not to move camera or background between the shooting sessions.

14. Have film processed.

15. Edit and splice animated movie.

16. Record background music and/or sound effects.

17. View and evaluate animated movie.

18. Discuss evaluation with class and teachers.

Evaluative Criteria: The students will plan and produce an animated movie.

LESSON 16

Title: P/S Sources.

Overview: The purpose of this lesson is to familiarize students with two sources of data: primary and secondary.

Library Media Skills Objective:

Identify primary and secondary sources.

Performance Objective: Given information on the classification of primary and secondary data, the students will identify primary and secondary sources.

Subject Area: Language Arts.

Learning Strategy: Discussion, practice.

Resources:

SIRS: Social Issues Resources Series Facts on File.

Jackdaw Kits.

McWhirter, Norris, and Ross McWhirter. *Guinness Book of Phenomenal Happenings.*

Newspapers.

Magazines.

Diaries.

Letters.

Pictures.

Contracts.

Historical novel.

History book.

Worksheet (see page 230).

Methods:

The teacher will:

1. Invite the library media specialist to come to the classroom to discuss primary and secondary sources of data.
2. Record grades from worksheet.
3. Evaluate lesson and review worksheet.

P/S Sources of Data

Write **P** if primary, **S** if secondary source of data.

Certificate

History book

Deed

Bible commentary

Will

Textbook

Charter

Government documents

Editorial

Law

Historical novel

Contract

Letters

Newspaper accounts

Time capsules

Magazine accounts

Diaries

Pictures

Constitutions

Methods (cont'd.)

The library media specialist will:

1. Gather samples of primary and secondary sources.
2. Ask students to define primary and secondary sources.
3. Discuss the space shuttle as a topic for research. What are some primary sources you could use? What are some secondary sources?
4. Give out worksheet.
5. Correct worksheet with students and discuss answers. Show examples.

The students will:

1. Define primary and secondary sources.
2. Discuss applications of primary and secondary sources.
3. Complete worksheet.
4. Discuss answers.

Evaluative Criteria: The students will correctly identify primary and secondary sources.

LESSON 17

Title: Is the Medium the Message?

Overview: The purpose of this unit on visual literacy is to help students understand the messages of visuals, develop visual skills, and communicate their own ideas through a visual and literary medium.

Library Media Skills Objectives:

Identify and use all parts of a book.

Infer facts and ideas from reading.

Evaluate material for appropriateness.

Locate specific information using a film, picture, or tape.

Summarize information from a visual and/or auditory stimulus.

Compare two sources of information.

Select suitable modes of production for presentations.

Performance Objective: Given information on visual literacy, activities to develop visual skills, and a visual literary project guide, the students will plan and produce a still photography project.

Subject Area: Language Arts.

Learning Strategy: Audiovisual instruction, lecture, learning centers, project.

Resources:

Slides: *Learning to See and Understand: Developing Visual Literacy.* The Center for Humanities.
Â Â Â Â Â Â Â *Creative Expression.* Society of Visual Education.

Filmstrips: Â *The Art of Seeing.* Warren Schloat.
Â Â Â Â Â Â Â Â Â Â Â Â *An Interview with Henry David Thoreau.* Scott, Foresman & Co.
Â Â Â Â Â Â Â Â Â Â Â Â *Images and Imagination: Seeing Creatively.* Eye Gate House.

Books: Pearson, John. *Begin Sweet World.*
Â Â Â Â Â Â Â Hopkins, Lee. *Moments.*
Â Â Â Â Â Â Â Lewis, Richard. *The Moment of Wonder.*
Â Â Â Â Â Â Â Deutsch, Babette. *Poetry Handbook: A Dictionary of Terms.*
Â Â Â Â Â Â Â McCormick, J. *The Life of the Forest.*
Â Â Â Â Â Â Â National Geographic Society. *Images of the World.*
Â Â Â Â Â Â Â Porter, Eliot. *In Wildness Is the Preservation of the World.*

Centers.

Visual Literacy Project Guidelines (see page 234).

Centers

Center 1: Read the preface, foreword, or introduction to the following books to determine the purpose of the author or editor:

    A. Porter, Eliot. *In Wildness Is the Preservation of the World.* Look at the photographs and read the text. The photographer has captured the message of Henry David Thoreau. Write a short, descriptive paragraph explaining the message.

    B. National Geographic. *Images of the World.* This book was produced by National Geographic photographers who have something to communicate. Look at the photographs and read the captions. Write a paragraph describing your impressions of these images.

Center 2: View and listen to Part I of *An Interview with Henry David Thoreau.* This sound filmstrip presents the essence of Thoreau's thoughts about life through quotations and illustrations. Write a brief summary of Thoreau's ideas. Are his ideas still pertinent today?

Center 3: View and listen to the sound filmstrip *The Art of Seeing—How to Use Your Eyes,* Part I. This filmstrip makes a distinction between looking and seeing. Write a paragraph discussing the difference between *looking* and *seeing.* Do you really *see* your environment? Draw a picture of the kitchen in your home from memory. Draw a picture of an area in the media center while you are "seeing" it.

Center 4: View the filmstrip *Bridges from Here to There.* Discuss with your group the questions asked in the filmstrip. Compare and contrast the architecture, design, and size of the bridges shown. Write a summary of your discussion.

Center 5: Look at the book *Begin Sweet World* and find the statement concerning the artist and the poet by Anais Nin. Select and read several poetry books. Match the numbered photographs in your packet with poems that are not illustrated. Copy the poems on a separate piece of paper and list the number of the picture you matched with the poem.

Center 6: Read the chapter *The Mass Media as Languages* in the booklet. Answer questions 1-3 on page 63.

Center 7: View the slide set *Faces and Feelings.* Use your imagination to convey your thoughts and feelings about the message you receive from the slides. Select one or more of the following ways to communicate your message:

    A. Arrange the slides in a sequence to tell a story.

    B. Write captions for the slides.

    C. Select music related to the theme you have chosen.

    D. Study the composition of several slides. Write a description of the use of color, contrast, shadows, camera angles, point-of-view.

Visual Literacy Project Guidelines

Work as a group to express yourself through still photography and a literary medium.

Ideas for literary medium

- Music
- Poetry
- Quotations
- Captions
- Short Story

Ideas for photography (Use prints or slides)

- Use 35-mm camera, indoors and outdoors.
- Use Kodak Visual Maker to copy pictures that are hand-drawn.
- Use write-on slides to draw pictures.
- Use prints from magazines or books.
- Use prepared slides from our collection.
- Use instant camera.

Plan your project.

1. Start with an idea.
2. Select the medium you will use.
3. Plan your objective—what you want to accomplish.
4. Make a storyboard.
5. Prepare visuals.
6. Use the talents of everyone in your group.
7. Take photographs (or use prepared slides or prints).
8. Combine photographs with literary medium.
9. View and evaluate.
10. Did you accomplish your purpose?

Methods:

The teacher will:

1. Use the teacher's guide to the slide program *Learning to See and Understand: Developing Visual Literacy* to plan activities for students before the presentation of the program.

2. Present the slide program, Parts I and II, and lead students in a discussion of the elements of a visual vocabulary, the types of visual expression, and the influences on vision and perception.

3. Ask the library media specialist to explain to the students the procedures for completing the learning center activities in the media center.

4. Divide the class into seven groups.

5. Accompany the students to the media center; rotate to each activity to give supervision.

6. Review and discuss the completed learning center activities with the library media specialist to determine grades for students.

7. Read the proposals for projects by students and discuss details with students.

8. Allow students to meet with the library media specialist for assistance with the photography projects.

9. View and evaluate projects with the library media specialist.

The library media specialist will:

1. Plan and develop the entire unit with the teacher.

2. Divide responsibilities with the teacher.

3. Write activities for learning centers.

4. Set up centers with necessary resources.

5. Share supervision with the teacher of students who are working at the centers by asking questions, reviewing answers, and guiding activities.

6. After the students have completed the learning center activities over a period of seven days, invite the class to come to the media center for a multimedia program on creative expression. The program will show ideas for student projects:
   a. Make slides by using pictures from books and magazines. Include slides of words such as: war, peace, hate, love, wealth, poverty. Play the selected music while showing the slides.
   b. Show hand-drawn slides on *Women in Maryland* made by students or show pictures drawn on write-on slides that have been prepared ahead of time.
   c. Show a series of enlarged and mounted photographs that express some aspect of nature, such as life at the seashore.

7. Demonstrate the use of the Kodak Visual Maker, the 35-mm camera, and an instant camera.

8. Give technical assistance to students in selecting the correct type of film, using the elements of composition, and making good use of light.

9. View and evaluate projects with the teacher.

10. Review and evaluate entire unit with teacher. Revise unit.

Methods (cont'd.)

The students will:

1. Complete seven learning centers.

2. Work in groups. Each group will spend one class period at each center on a rotating schedule.

3. After completing the learning center activities and seeing the teacher's and library media specialist's evaluation, communicate their own ideas through still photography and a literary medium.

Evaluative Criteria: The students will successfully complete the activities in the seven learning centers. The written assignments will be graded on (1) spelling, (2) grammar, and (3) content. The students will create and present a still photography project. The project will be evaluated on

1. originality of theme.
2. organization.
3. focus.
4. photographic composition.
5. literary elements.
6. sound track.
7. general effectiveness.

LESSON 18

Title: Fun with Math.

Overview: The purpose of this lesson is to provide an opportunity for advanced math students to participate in independent research activities in the library media center.

Library Media Skills Objectives:

Determine appropriate sources for locating specific information.

Compare two sources of information.

Summarize information from a visual and/or auditory stimulus.

Draw appropriate conclusions based on information presented.

Determine adequacy of information.

Organize to show sequence.

Interpret specialized reference materials to develop and support research.

Utilize organization skills to produce a research product or media production.

Define a problem for research.

Performance Objectives: Given a list of suggested math-related activities, the student will select and complete one or more activities.

Subject Area: Math.

Learning Strategy: Independent study, project.

Resources:

Articles: "Numeration Systems and Numbers." *Compton's Encyclopedia.*

Books: Bell, E. T. *Men of Mathematics.*
St. John, Glory. *How to Count like a Martian.*
Adler, Peggy. *Math Puzzles.*
Linn, Charles. *The Age of Mathematics.*
Asimov, Isaac. *The Realm of Numbers.*
Fixx, James. *Solve It!*
Morgenstein, Steve. *Metric Puzzles, Tricks & Games.*
Summers, George. *Mind Teasers.*

Filmstrips: *Exploring Math Games and Diversions.* Guidance Associates.
Numbers: From Notches to Numerals. Center for the Humanities.

Methods:

The teacher will:

1. Identify math students who are performing above grade level and have demonstrated the ability and desire to work on an independent math project.

2. Meet with the library media specialist to discuss math topics for research and the availability of resources.

3. Meet with the students to discuss a schedule for conferences.

4. Review progress of student at specified conferences.

5. Evaluate project or report of students.

6. Review and evaluate independent study program with the library media specialist.

The library media specialist will:

1. Provide resources to plan math-related activities with the teacher.

2. Discuss research methods with students.

3. Schedule independent study time in media center with student.

4. Reserve materials and/or space for student.

5. Assist student with research and project by locating information, asking questions to clarify ideas, making suggestions, and providing technical assistance with equipment.

The student will select from the following activities:

1. Review the history of different numeration systems throughout the world and develop his or her own numeration system.

2. Solve interesting mathematical puzzles and make a puzzle for a bulletin board.

3. Choose three famous mathematicians and prepare a biographical sketch about each by producing a slide/tape, filmstrip, recording, video tape, or booklet.

4. Study the ideas behind the theorems of mathematics. Devise his or her own theorems and present them in an illustrated booklet or a series of charts.

5. Choose one of the branches of mathematics and learn more about it. Locate and use print and nonprint materials. Make notes and summarize the information. Compare and contrast the sources of information. Discuss the findings with math teacher.

6. Make a super 8-mm movie to illustrate a single mathematical concept.

Evaluative Criteria: The student will successfully complete one or more math-related activities.

LESSON 19

Title: Ready, Aim, Shoot!

Overview: The purpose of the lesson is to present basic information on photography in a mini-course. Students who are interested in learning more about photography are invited to join the photography club.

Library Media Skills Objectives:

Use an instant or 35-mm camera to take photographs and slides.

Select appropriate film for photographs and slides.

Performance Objective: Given an instant and/or a 35-mm camera and film, the students will take one or more prints or slides using good camera techniques.

Subject Area: Minicourse.

Learning Strategy: Demonstration, practice.

Resources:

Instant cameras.

35-mm cameras.

Instant film: color and black-and-white.

35-mm film: color slides, color prints, black-and-white.

Processing mailers.

Examples of photographs and slides.

Camera manuals.

Sound/slide series: *Photography Skills: Basics from the Eastman Kodak Company.* Unit 1: *The Beginnings of Photographic Composition;* Unit 2: *Basic Picture-Taking Techniques;* Unit 3: *Film: How It Works.* The Center for the Humanities.

Books: Langford, Michael. *The Step-by-Step Guide to Photography.*

Giambarba, Paul. *How to Make Better Polaroid Instant Pictures.*

Moldvay, Albert. *National Geographic Photographer's Field Guide.*

Glubok, Shirley. *The Art of Photography.*

Pamphlets: Eastman Kodak Company. *Photo Explorations AT-16.*

Picture-Taking AC-2.

Methods:

The library media specialist will:

1. Be responsible for teaching the minicourse.
2. During the first session, present the objectives and determine the entry level of each student.
3. Ask students to submit questions on basic photography.
4. Revise the content of the minicourse to meet the needs and abilities of the students.
5. Use the sound/slide program on photography skills from Eastman Kodak as a springboard for discussion and demonstration.
6. Guide students in the basics of camera handling: battery installation, loading of film, focusing, exposure, and holding camera steady.
7. Describe the elements of composition emphasizing the center of interest and point of view.
8. Take students outdoors for picture-taking sessions.
9. Have film developed.
10. Evaluate prints and slides with students.
11. Encourage interested students to join the photography club.

The students will:

1. Attend the photography minicourse sessions.
2. Bring own camera, if possible.
3. Assess background knowledge and level of experience with photography.
4. Write questions for inclusion in minicourse.
5. Practice basics of camera handling without film in camera.
6. Find pictures in magazines that demonstrate good composition.
7. Use instant and/or 35-mm camera to produce prints or slides.
8. Evaluate prints and slides.

Evaluative Criteria: The students will correctly use an instant and/or a 35-mm camera to produce prints or slides.

LESSON 20

Title: I Think I Can: Computer Programming.

Overview: The purpose of this unit is to provide information on programming languages for students who are interested in writing computer programs.

Library Media Skills Objectives:

Interpret information found in resources.

Compare and contrast facts from more than one source.

Performance Objectives: Given information on programming languages, the students will design and make a chart comparing and contrasting each language, listing strengths and weaknesses of each language.

Subject Area: Computer Club.

Learning Strategy: Group project.

Resources:

Programming Course: *Step-by-Step.* Program Design.

Apple Pilot. Apple Distributors.

Logo. Logo Computer Systems, Inc.

Filmstrip: *Understanding the Computer.* Sunburst.

Books: Albrecht, Robert, Leroy Finkel, and Jerald Brown. *Basic.* 2d ed.

Papert, Seymour. *Mindstorms: Children, Computers, and Powerful Ideas.*

Taylor, Robert, ed. *The Computer in the School: Tutor, Tutee, Tool.*

Smith, Brian R. *Introduction to Computer Programming.*

D'Ignazio, Fred. *Small Computers: Exploring Their Technology and Future.*

Magazine Articles: Bussey, Jim. "Logo: A Language for Everyone." *Commodore: The Microcomputer Magazine* (May 1983): 43-45.

Blank, George. "Tourist's Guide to the Cybernetic Tower of Babel (languages)." *Creative Computing* (Nov. 1981): 94-103.

Lindsay, Len. "Choosing a Programming Language to Teach in School." *Commodore: The Microcomputer Magazine* (May 1983): 48-51.

Microcomputers: APPLE, PET, ATARI, IBM PC, TRS-80 (if available).

Software: *Apple Logo.* Logo Computer Systems, Inc.

Atari Writer. Atari, Inc.

Apple Writer II. Apple Computer, Inc.

Bank Street Writer. Broderbund Software.

Methods:

The teacher (club sponsor) will:

1. Organize a computer club to meet during lunch, at activity period, or after school one day a week.

2. Ask library media specialist to reserve computer resource materials for use by club members.

3. Introduce programming languages by reviewing LOGO, BASIC, and PILOT.

4. Allow small groups of students to use the programming courses *Step-by-Step* and *Apple Pilot* during several club sessions.

5. Invite the library media specialist to talk about computer resources dealing with programming languages.

6. Ask students to design and make a large chart listing programming languages.

7. Let students compare and contrast each language they learn about and add information to the chart.

8. Invite students, former students, teachers, parents, or computer experts to tell about and demonstrate use of PASCAL, COBOL, FORTRAN, COMAL, and others.

9. Review and discuss information on chart. Make necessary changes. Make a new chart to display in the computer center in the library media center.

The library media specialist will:

1. Learn about computers and programming languages.

2. Build a strong resource collection of computer material.

3. Reserve a collection of materials for use by computer club members and sponsor.

4. Obtain programming courses: *Step-by-Step* and *Apple Pilot.*

5. Prepare and present talk to computer club on resources dealing with programming languages.

6. Assist club sponsor in locating resource people.

7. Laminate and display completed chart on programming languages.

The students will:

1. Join computer club.

2. Take active part in club's activities.

3. Learn about programming languages from computer resource materials and from resource people.

4. Interpret information.

5. Compare and contrast facts from more than one source.

6. Design and make a chart of programming languages listing strengths and weaknesses of each language.

7. Learn at least one new programming language and write a computer program. (optional)

Evaluative Criteria: The students will complete a chart of programming languages listing strengths and weaknesses.

LESSON 21

Title: Fiesta Español!

Overview: The purpose of this lesson is to introduce students to Spanish holidays. They will choose a holiday and present an oral report on it.

Library Media Skills Objectives:

Select a reference source.

Organize information around a topic.

Infer facts from maps, charts, graphs.

Performance Objective: Given a worksheet, the students will select a Spanish holiday, locate information about the holiday, organize a report, and present an oral report.

Subject Area: Spanish.

Learning Strategy: Discussion, practice.

Resources:

Putnam's Contemporary Spanish Dictionary: Spanish-English; Inglés-Español.

Dobler, Lavinia. *National Holidays around the World.*

Pei, Mario. *Talking Your Way around the World.*

Worksheet (see page 244).

Methods:

The teacher will:
1. Prepare a worksheet on Spanish holidays.
2. Discuss the objectives.
3. Schedule small groups of students to work in the library media center.
4. Assess the oral reports.

The library media specialist will:
1. Reserve resources.
2. Assist students in locating information.
3. Attend the oral presentations.

The students will:
1. Select a Spanish holiday for a report.
2. Locate, select, and interpret appropriate resources.
3. Utilize maps and charts.
4. Prepare and present oral report.

Evaluative Criteria: The students will successfully complete the assignment and present an oral report on a Spanish holiday.

Worksheet
Fiesta Español!

Select one of the following topics and prepare an oral report:

Las Navidades   El Día de los Santos Inocentes

La Nochevieja   Las Reyes Magos

La Santa Semana   Las Ferias

Include the following in Spanish:

Greetings and salutations

Dates

Expressions

You may use visual aids for your report.

LESSON 22

Title: Moving On!

Overview: The purpose of this activity is to hold a festival for eighth-grade students to allow them to view and evaluate media productions in which they participated or which they created during their three years as a middle school student.

Library Media Skills Objectives:

Evaluate media productions.

Performance Objectives: Given criteria for evaluating media productions, the students will evaluate and critique selected media productions.

Subject Area: Social Studies.

Learning Strategy: Audiovisual presentation, evaluation.

Resources:

Examples of student media productions:
Super 8-mm movies: *The Day the School Disappeared.*
Vandalism.
Slide tapes: *The Assassinated Presidents.*
Video Games.
Friendship.
The World Aflame.
Video tapes: *Commercials.*
The Classics.
The Beatles.
Speeches.
Debates.
News Quiz Show.
Gymnastics.
Career Interviews.
Let's Visit Asia.
Audio tapes: *The Shadow.*

Criteria for Evaluating Media Productions.

Program for Media Festival.

Posters.

Popcorn.

Methods:

The teacher will:

1. Ask students to list the media productions in which they participated or which they created in their three years as a middle school student. Give list to the library media specialist.
2. Plan with the library media specialist to arrange a program for student viewing.
3. Arrange to show a movie to students not participating in the media festival.
4. Give students a program for the media festival.

The library media specialist will:

1. Locate video tapes requested by students by checking video log.
2. Check the student productions' file for super 8-mm movies, slides, tapes, and audio tapes.
3. Schedule screenings.
4. List location and time of screening with titles of productions in a program for the media festival.
5. Give programs to the teacher to distribute.
6. Prepare posters for display, advertising students' productions.
7. Invite parents to attend the festival.
8. Give out small bags of popcorn to audience.
9. Ask students to complete the evaluation form for each production they view.
10. Collect and review evaluation forms.

The students will:

1. List the media productions in which they participated during three years as a middle school student.
2. Check festival program for screening times.
3. Invite parents to attend festival.
4. View and evaluate productions.

Evaluative Criteria: The students will view and evaluate media productions.

9
Selected Resources

PRINT (Books)

Alfred Hitchcock's Tales to Fill You with Fear and Trembling. Eleanor Sullivan, ed. New York: Dial Press, 1980.

Alfred Hitchcock's Witch's Brew. Alfred Hitchcock, ed. Westminster, Md.: Random House, 1977.

Almanac of Dates. Linda Millgate. New York: Harcourt Brace Jovanovich, Inc., 1977.

The American Heritage History of the 20's and 30's. New York: American Heritage Publishing Company, 1970.

The Art of Photography. Shirley Glubok. New York: Macmillan Publishing Company, 1977.

Asimov's Guide to Shakespeare. Issac Asimov. Garden City, N.Y.: Doubleday, 1970.

Atlas of Man. New York: St. Martin's Press, Inc., 1978.

Buffalo Kill. G. D. Christensen. New York: Archway Paperbacks, 1968.

Careers Encyclopedia. Craig Norback. Homewood, Ill.: Dow Jones-Irwin, 1980.

Computers in Mathematics: A Sourcebook of Ideas. David Ahl. Morristown, N.J.: Creative Computing, 1980.

The Constellations, How They Came to Be. Roy Gallant. New York: Four Winds Press, 1979.

Dictionary of Astronomy, Space and Atmospheric Phenomena. David Tver. New York: Van Nostrand Rheinhold Company, 1979.

Dupper. Betty Baker. New York: William Morrow and Company, 1976.

Eight Black American Inventors. Robert Hayden. Reading, Mass.: Addison-Wesley Publishing Co., Inc., 1972.

Facts about the Fifty States. Sue Brandt. New York: Franklin Watts, Inc., 1970.

Facts on File. New York: Facts on File, Inc.

Field Guide to Rocks and Minerals. 4th ed. Frederick H. Pough. Boston: Houghton Mifflin Co., 1978.

French Cooking in Ten Minutes. Edouard de Pomiane. New York: Atheneum Publishers, 1979.

Gentlehands. M. E. Kerr. New York: Bantam Books, Inc., 1981.

Good for Me. Marilyn Burns. Boston: Little, Brown & Co., 1978.

The Great Brain Does It Again. John Fitzgerald. New York: Dial Press, 1975.

The Great Jazz Artists. James Collier. New York: Four Winds Press, 1977.

Heavens Above! Heather Couper and Terence Murtagh. New York: Franklin Watts, Inc., 1981.

Heraclea: A Legend of Warrior Women. Bernard Evslin. Englewood Cliffs, N.J.: Scholastic Book Services, 1978.

How to Be an Inventor. Harvey Weiss. New York: Thomas Y. Crowell Company, 1980.

How to Give a Speech. Henry Gilford. New York: Franklin Watts, Inc., 1980.

Hunter's Stew and Hangtown Fry. Lila Perl. New York: Seabury Press, Inc., 1977.

Images of the World. Washington, D.C.: National Geographic Society, 1981.

Incredible Journey. Shelia Burnford. Boston: Little, Brown & Co., 1961.

Indian Corn and Other Gifts. Sigmund Lavine. New York: Dodd, Mead and Company, 1974.

Jacob Have I Loved. Katherine Paterson. New York: Avon Books, 1981.

Jupiter. Franklyn Branley. New York: E. P. Dutton, 1981.

Many Hands Cooking. Terry Cooper and Marilyn Ratner. New York: Thomas Y. Crowell Company, 1974.

Media Magic. Mary Margrabe. Washington, D.C.: Acropolis Books, 1979.

Mindstorms: Children, Computers, and Powerful Ideas. Seymour Papert. New York: Basic Books, Inc., 1980.

Mr. Popper's Penguins. Richard Atwater and Florence Atwater. Boston: Little, Brown & Co., 1938.

Mythologies of the World: A Concise Encyclopedia. Max Shapiro, ed. Garden City, N.Y.: Doubleday and Company, Inc., 1979.

Mythology. Edith Hamilton. Boston: Little, Brown & Co., 1942.

Myths. Alexander Eliot. New York: McGraw-Hill Book Company, 1976.

National Geographic Photographer's Field Guide. Albert Moldvay. Washington, D.C.: National Geographic Society, 1981.

National Geographic Picture Atlas of Our Fifty States. Washington, D.C.: National Geographic Society, 1980.

National Geographic Picture Atlas of Our World. Washington, D.C.: National Geographic Society, 1979.

New Encyclopedia of Sports. Ralph Hickok. New York: McGraw-Hill Book Company, 1977.

Occupational Outlook Handbook, 1982-83. Washington, D.C.: U.S. Government Printing Office, 1983.

Picture Atlas of Our Universe. Washington, D.C.: National Geographic Society, 1980.

Quasars, Pulsars and Black Holes. Melvin Berger. New York: G. P. Putnam and Sons, 1977.

Rand McNally Cosmopolitan World Atlas. Chicago: Rand McNally, 1978.

Sign Language. Laura Greene and Eva Dicker. New York: Franklin Watts, Inc., 1981.

Small Computers: Exploring Their Technology and Future. Fred D'Ignazio. New York: Franklin Watts, Inc., 1981.

Social Issues Resource Series. Boca Raton, Fla.: Social Issues Research Series, Inc., 1982.

Soup for President. Robert Peck. New York: Alfred A. Knopf, Inc., 1978.

Those Inventive Americans. Washington, D.C.: National Geographic Society, 1971.

To Look at Anything. Lee Hopkins. New York: Harcourt Brace Jovanovich, Inc., 1978.

Venus, Near Neighbor of the Sun. Isaac Asimov. West Caldwell, N.J.: William Morrow and Company, 1981.

The Washington Post. Carol Williams. Englewood Cliffs, N.J.: Prentice-Hall, Inc., 1976.

Watership Down. Richard Adams. New York: Macmillan, 1972.

Webster's Biographical Dictionary. Springfield, Mass.: G. and C. Merriam Company, 1971.

Wierd and Wacky Inventions. Jim Murphy. New York: Crown Publishers, Inc., 1978.

What Computers Can't Do: The Limits of Artificial Intelligence. rev. ed. Herbert Drefus. New York: Harper & Row, 1979.

Working with Words. Margaret Harmon. Philadelphia: Westminster Press, 1977.

World Almanac and Book of Facts. New York: World Almanac.

NONPRINT

FILMS (16-mm)

Animation Pie. San Francisco, Calif.: Palmer Film Services, 1975.

Claymation. New York: Billy Budd Films, Inc., 1978.

Decisions, Decisions. Los Angeles: Churchill Films, 1973.

Effective Writing: Research Skills. Chicago: Coronet Films, 1972.

The Reference Section. Pasadena, Calif.: Barr Films, 1980.

FILMS (8-mm)

Optical Illusion. Chicago: Encyclopaedia Britannica Educational Corp., 1968.

Planetary Motions. Chicago: Encyclopaedia Britannica Educational Corp., 1971.

Solar System. Chicago: Encyclopaedia Britannica Educational Corp., 1971.

GAMES

Dewey Dotto #1. Dewey Dotto #2. Marietta, Ga.: Larlin Corporation, 1976.

Information Fast! Inglewood, Calif.: Educational Insights, Inc., 1974.

Fact and Opinion. Paoli, Penn.: Instructo, 1975.

Search and Research. New York: Educational Activities, 1981.

KITS

Age of Exploration and Discovery. Chicago: Coronet Films, 1975.

Astronomy. Washington, D.C.: National Geographic Society, 1978.

Black Folk Music in America. Chicago: Society for Visual Education, Inc., 1970.

Choosing the Medium. Chicago: Encyclopaedia Britannica Corp., 1974.

Dinosaurs. Washington, D.C.: National Geographic Society, 1978.

Food for the World. Washington, D.C.: National Geographic Society, 1976.

Great Explorers. Washington, D.C.: National Geographic Society, 1978.

Japan: Economic Miracle. Chicago: Encyclopaedia Britannica Educational Corp., 1974.

Lands and People of Asia. Washington, D.C.: National Geographic Society, 1972.

Livelyhoods: Your Lifestyle. Boston: Houghton Mifflin Co., 1979.

Media Organization: Nonfiction. Chicago: Encyclopaedia Britannica Educational Corp., 1974.

Myths of Greece and Rome. Chicago: Society for Visual Education, Inc., 1978.

Mythology Lives! Ancient Stories and Modern Literature. Mt. Kisco, N.Y.: Center for the Humanities, 1982.

Now Hear This! Becoming a Better Listener. Mt. Kisco, N.Y.: Center for the Humanities, 1980.

A Pocketful of Poetry. Mt. Kisco, N.Y.: Guidance Associates, 1974.

Spiderman. New York: McGraw-Hill, Inc., 1975.

Understanding Poetry. Chicago: Society for Visual Education, Inc., 1979.

Understanding the Computer. Pleasantville, N.Y.: Sunburst Communications, 1981.

The Universe. Washington, D.C.: National Geographic Society, 1972.

The World of Media. Chicago: Encyclopaedia Britannica Educational Corp., 1974.

MICROCOMPUTER SOFTWARE

Almanacs. St. Louis, Mo.: Calico, 1981.

Apple Writer II. Cupertino, Calif.: Apple Computer, Inc., 1982.

Bank Street Writer. New York: Scholastic, Inc., 1981.

Cells. Freeport, N.Y.: Educational Activities, 1982.

Dragon Games. Freeport, N.Y.: Educational Activities, 1982.

Introduction to Computers. Chicago: Society for Visual Education, Inc., 1981.

Math Sequences. St. Louis, Mo.: Milliken Publishing Company, 1980.

Moptown. Portola Valley, Calif.: Advanced Learning Technology, 1981.

TAPES (AUDIO)

Are You Listening? New York: J C Penney Company, Inc., 1971.

Heroes, Gods, and Monsters. Old Greenwich, Conn.: Spoken Arts, 1971.

Short Stories of O. Henry. Old Greenwich, Conn.: Spoken Arts, 1971.

Understanding the Newspaper. Chicago: Coronet, 1975.

TRANSPARENCIES

Basic Dictionary Skills. St. Louis, Mo.: Milliken Publishing Company, 1973.

Basic Library Skills. St. Louis, Mo.: Milliken Publishing Company, 1973.

Reference Study Skills. Chicago: Encyclopaedia Britannica Educational Corp., 1969.

LIST OF VENDORS

Addison-Wesley Publishing Company, Inc.
Jacob Way
Reading, MA 01867

American Heritage Publishing Company
10 Rockefeller Plaza
New York, NY 10021

Apple Computer, Inc.
20525 Mariana Ave.
Cupertino, CA 95014

Atheneum Publishers
597 Fifth Ave.
New York, NY 10017

Avon Books
959 Eighth Ave.
New York, NY 10019

Bantam Books, Inc.
666 Fifth Ave.
New York, NY 10019

Barr Films
Box 5667
Pasadena, CA 91107

Basic Books, Inc.
10 East 53rd Street
New York, NY 10022

Billy Budd Films
235 East 57th Street
New York, NY 10022

CALICO, Inc.
P. O. Box 15916
St. Louis, MO 63114

Center for the Humanities
Communications Park
Box 3000
Mount Kisco, NY 10549

Churchill Films
662 North Robertson Boulevard
Los Angeles, CA 90069

Coronet Films
65 E. South Water Street
Chicago, IL 60602

Creative Computing
P. O. Box 789M
Morristown, NJ 07960

Thomas Y. Crowell Company
10 E. 53rd Street
New York, NY 10022

Crown Publishers, Inc.
1 Park Avenue
New York, NY 10016

Dial Press
1 Dag Hammarskjold Plaza
245 East 47th Street
New York, NY 10017

Dow Jones-Irwin
1818 Ridge Road
Homewood, IL 60430

Dodd, Mead and Company
79 Madison Ave.
New York, NY 10016

Doubleday and Company, Inc.
501 Franklin Avenue
Garden City, NY 11530

E. P. Dutton and Company
2 Park Ave.
New York, NY 10016

Educational Activities
Box 392
Freeport, NY 11520

Educational Insights
Department T
211 S. Hindry Ave.
Inglewood, CA 90301

Facts on File, Inc.
460 Park Ave. S.
New York, NY 10016

Government Printing Office
710 N. Capitol Street
Washington, DC 20402

Guidance Associates
Communications Park
Box 3000
Mount Kisco, NY 10549

Houghton Mifflin Company
2 Park Street
Boston, MA 02107

Instructo Corporation
Paoli, PA 19301

Alfred A. Knopf, Inc.
201 E. 50th Street
New York, NY 10022

Libraries Unlimited, Inc.
P. O. Box 263
Littleton, CO 80160

Little, Brown and Company
34 Beacon Street
Boston, MA 02106

McGraw-Hill Book Company
1221 Avenue of the Americas
New York, NY 10020

Macmillan Publishing Company, Inc.
866 Third Avenue
New York, NY 10022

G. and C. Merriam Company
47 Federal Street
Springfield, MA 01101

Milliken Publishing Company
1100 Research Road
St. Louis, MO 63132

William Morrow and Company, Inc.
105 Madison Ave.
New York, NY 10016

National Geographic Society
17th and M Streets, N.W.
Washington, DC 20036

Prentice-Hall, Inc.
Box 500
Englewood Cliffs, NJ 07632

G. P. Putnam and Sons
200 Madison Ave.
New York, NY 10016

St. Martin's Press, Inc.
175 Fifth Ave.
New York, NY 10010

Scholastic, Inc.
730 Broadway
New York, NY 10003

Seabury Press, Inc.
815 Second Ave.
New York, NY 10017

Society for Visual Education, Inc.
1345 Diversey Parkway
Chicago, IL 60614

Sunburst Communications
41 Washington Ave.
Pleasantville, NY 10570

Franklin Watts, Inc.
730 Fifth Ave.
New York, NY 10019

Westminster Press
925 Chestnut Street
Philadelphia, PA 19107

Index